Scared Boys, Terrified Men:

Approaching the Healing of Male Childhood Sexual Abuse from a Faith & Psychological Perspective

Thomas Edward

Scripture quotations are from The Classic Reference Edition, English Standard Version® (ESV®) Copyright © 2001 by Crossway Bibles, a publishing ministry of Good News Publishers All rights reserved.

Copyright © 2012 Thomas Edward

All rights reserved. No part of this publication may be reproduced, stored in a retrieval system, or transmitted in any form or by any means, electronic, mechanical, photocopying, recording, or otherwise, without the prior written permission of the publisher.

ISBN: 978-1-60383-441-4

Published by:
Holy Fire Publishing
PO Box 540693
Merritt Island, FL 32954

www.ChristianPublish.com

Printed in the United States of America and the United Kingdom

Table of Contents

Preface 7
The Narrow Way 9

Chapter One 13
  Don't Miss This 13
    What to Expect 14
    Your Life Sucks 16
    Where to Turn 17
    Let's Get Personal 19
    Mixing Spiritual and Psychological? 21

Chapter Two 25
  Hard Questions 25
    Is this Reality? 25
    Are Believers Immune? 27
    Was I Abused? 28
    Any Signs I May Have Been Abused? 33
    Emotional Abuse 35
    What Forms of Sexual Abuse? 42
    Why Was I So Naive? 44
    Myths about Abusers 46

Chapter Three 57
  Family Hurts 57
    How Has It Shaped Your View? 60
    A Friend 65
    What's Holding You Back? 71
    Society Plays a Part 73
    Common Obstacles 75
    Disclosure 76
    Loved Ones Asked: How can I help him? 83

Chapter Four 89
  Trapped 89
    What did I lose? 91
    Loss Childhood 92

Lies Destroys...95
Making Excuses is Easier...102
Flashbacks 115
Why Do They Feel So Real?.......................................117
Flashbacks Make Me Sexless.....................................119
Continual Tears 119
When Love Is on the Line!...120

Chapter Five 131
  Sex and Identity 131
    Sex Is a Bad Word...131
    Internal Messages..132
    Perspective 133
    Sexuality, Shame and Confusion 144
    Intimacy...150
    Abuse and Excitement...153
    In your brain 155
    Manly Images..167
    Are Men Always Strong..172
    Struggling Masculinity..174

Chapter Six..185
  Healing 185
    To Tell...187
    Why not Isolation?..189
    Transforming the Worst to the Best 190
    Healing Takes Time 191
    Recovery Is Real but You Need Help.......................196
    Facing Feelings 199
    Vocabulary to Express Feelings................................201
    Building up Defenses 208
    Recover and Reclaim 215

Chapter Seven 229
  Working through Issues 229
    Does Vulnerability Equal Weakness?.......................229
    Have This Attitude 232
    Judas Feelings: Suicide 235
    Sharing an Experience..236

Moving Through Stages...240
Therapy Isn't a Bad Word..245
Confronting the Abuser..247
Forgiveness or Vengeance 250
In Relationship with a God I Don't Know Yet 253

A Final Word 261

References...263

Preface

The air buzzed with whispers as the church members awaited the arrival of the speaker. The senior and associate pastor blitzed down the aisle to meet me in the foyer. The senior pastor panted. "I'm glad to meet you! Our associate pastor here made a mistake. He forgot to check with me before proceeding to invite you to speak on this subject. I don't think… I mean, we don't think it would be an appropriate subject to expose the congregation to at this time." The associate pastor apologized. They escorted me back through the entry doors. Looking puzzled I asked, "Are you sure? What if a parent, spouse, family or church member can benefit? The people are already here!" Two months later I received a call from a mother in that congregation. "My college son overdosed several weeks ago. He was almost successful. We found out that he was sexual abused. He's really having issue and we cannot find help or resources for men. I'm told your ministry helps Christian men who are dealing with the aftermath of childhood sexual abuse and molestation. Can you help?"

Although believed to be higher, the number of reported cases of sexually abused boys is 1 of 6. That would suggest that 10-20% or millions of boys are living with a devastating secret. Now envision this young boy as an adult man ten, twenty or thirty years later. He's there as a husband, father, or friend among the members in the congregation. He's struggling to emotionally cope and deal with the aftermath of the secret of his abuse. His wife, family and church friends notice his tendency to isolate himself. He is tortured inwardly. He's plagued by false guilt, shame and unresolved grief. He fights a battle that he cannot win alone. He struggles leading a double life because he cannot divulge the secret. "Pray more! Be more active!" are the magical mantras touted from the pulpits that are supposed to exorcise these demons from his life. The reality of these mantras exposes our timidity to confront such issues, to ignore their existence. It's not a cold calculating intentional disregard, but fear and neglect. It's a neglect that leads us to deny and ignore the reality that Christians get stuck too.

The Narrow Way

Some days its so difficult trying to walk this faith, attempting to show brotherly love to people whose attitudes are like those of the Pharisees. I can only imagine the venoms looks and the scandalous whispers spoken behind Jesus' back as he ministered to the, adulterers, , tax collectors, demon-possessed, exhortioners, the Samaritan woman, Mary Magadelene, the people who did not fit into the self-righteous traditional views of the religious right. The people who forgot that their righteousness according to Isaiah was as filthy rags before the Father. A friend shared with me his experience as male survivor advocate attending a Christian college conference where they were allowed a booth. They passed out literature for helping male survivors to find resources and help in dealing with the abuse. Dare I even say what the main conflating issue for ministers, pastors, elders, attending members. It was homosexuality. My heart stopped when I heard the news. Like those during Jesus' day, they totally missed the picture by focusing on their own discomfort, instead of seeing hurting people created in the image of God. Only certain people warrant the mercy, compassion and help of God. Those who look like us and act exactly like us! Somewhere in the greater picture they missed the scripture that states .."and such were some of you."

Now disseminate that fearful attitude across the churches in this nation and answer this question, "How many men of faith who are hurting and struggling with the long-terms effects of childhood sexual abuse will dare to step forward and ask for help?" Not many. No problem! We would help if it were alcoholism, divorce, anger management, suicide, domestic violence, infidelity, compulsive behaviors, substance abuse, run-away teens? Seeing the different celebrate recovery and alcohol programs, I would probably say, Yes. What if the issues mentioned above were manifested symptoms of a deeper root issue, like childhood sexual abuse? That's what I experience at the faith-based workshops I conduct. As a survivor myself, my heart goes out to other male survivors of faith who must fight this battle. We must endure a battle where in the mind of various believers the sexual crime committed against us makes us the criminal carrying the shame, guilt and betrayal. To acknowledge this reality is a death sentence in many Christian circles. They often conflate the sexual abuse with homosexuality as they fight a popular socio-political topic of our day. However, my prayer is that you do not give up! It's time to start living. I often wondered why Jesus said that "narrow is the way" and when I see how He loved people with "a new commandment I give you to love one another as I have loved you" I start to understand what He meant. When I start seeing the sacrifice He made in His own life to help others, the downcast, trodden, misfits, hurting, the imperfect, I begin to understand how narrow or difficult it is to love like this. Then when I see Him hanging on a cross with abuses, insults, despair, anger hurled at Him from the creatures He created and He still gives His life, I get the picture. I see the

"Lay a firm foundation with the bricks that others throw at you."
-David Brinkley

narrow way! My encounters attempting to bring this ministry to others has not yet resulted in crucifixion, thank God ☺ . However, it has produced insults, anger, abuses and being ostracize from those who don't understand. God has allowed me this small act of love, to use my desire to help other struggling men facing these issues. May that small act of love be considered a path on the narrow way!

Chapter One
Don't Miss This

And He called a child to Himself and set him before them, "And whoever receives one such child in My name receives Me; but whoever causes one of these little ones who believe in Me to stumble, it would be better for him to have a heavy millstone hung around his neck, and to be drowned in the depth of the sea.   Matthew 18:5-6

Have you ever felt like an inadequate novice? Three years ago, when I wrote my first book to help male survivors of childhood sexual abuse in the faith community, I was not ready for the backlash and rejection. Why write the second installment? (1) Because the struggles these past years have illuminated the words expressed to me by a New Life Ministries counselor. "Don't give up, so when the Christian community finally awakens to this problem resources for these men will be readily available" (2) and seeing the transformed lives of these men and their families totally outweighs the flack received for discussing taboo topics in Christian circles. If you are reading this book as a survivor, friend, or Christian counselor of a man who has been sexually abused, I hope the information contained on these pages will help in providing assistance on your personal journey as a survivor or a loved one helping another to deal with the pain of the sexual abuse.

What to Expect

If you or a man you loved was sexually abused as a child this book is for you. If you are reading this book perhaps you are ready for another stage. I wrote it because I want to encourage you, and cheer you on. I want to mourn with you, weep with you, laugh with you, and challenge you to grow. I share with you how God's truths and promises and psychological understandings worked powerfully in my life and others to heal the pain. Use this book as a tool to battle the dark demons and negative short and long-term effects of the unwanted abusive sexual experience. Perhaps you are searching for answers to heal. You want to restore the life, joy, happiness and confidence stolen by the treachery of childhood sexual abuse. You are longing to learn from others who have experienced the abuse and from others who have emerged from the murky pits of shame, false guilt, and embarrassment. Maybe you are working with a counselor, a faith-based therapist, a member of a recovery group and finally confronting the reality of your abuse. Maybe you feel like damaged goods, and you want to replace your broken self-esteem with confidence. I wrote this book for you. You may not feel like a hero but in my book you are. It will take strength, to admit vulnerabilities and face the pain. It will take courage to change unhealthy behavior patterns that worked as a child, but now create dysfunctional living in adulthood. You must do something! You will naturally resist because pain and discomfort will be part of the wilderness experience. However, like the children of Israel you must embrace the wilderness journey to reach your promised land. Realize that you cannot do it alone! You must fight the impulse to be a lone ranger, not even God does it alone, are we more powerful than He. You must share the struggle. This complicaed topic can be very overwhelming. I have learned from conducting workshops to present information in small bites. This book is not designed to hit every aspect one may encounter, but it does address some of the basics. Some of the stories in this book are from the lives of men who have attended the workshops and have worked to overcome these struggles. Some of the stories are my own. Please understand that the names and other identifying details have been omitted to protect the privacy of these individuals. The stories include examples of men shattering the silence, sharing the power of the abuse, and the power of healing. They represent the voice of millions of others like you who have suffered sexual abuse. Here's a stat for you. Although believed to be higher, the number of sexually abused men is 1in 6.

Using this book

Included are scriptures, principles, prayers and practices that have helped other men to heal. It's about what God can do for those who are willing to be open. Use the sections of the book as you are ready to address them. But don't just read the sections. Act on it! Healing is hard work. The principle true that you harvest what you plant. Therefore start planting so you can reap the benefits. You will be asked to write down your thoughts, feelings, and ideas. You will also be asked to read, pray, reflect and discuss. Trust me, if you do the work it will be more rewarding. Also I must apologize upfront. This subject is so vast it's difficult to start at the beginning and anyone who knows me understands my limited attention span. Okay, I'll cite my TBI (traumatic brain injury from being run over by a car several years ago) for the short attention span when writing. However if the generalization is true that men don't enjoy reading long drawn out paragraphs, but short burst of text, this will work. Secondly, this book is not a treatment book and not intended to replace therapy or counseling, but an advocate. Biblically an advocate is one who comes alongside to assist. So let's get started.

Your Life Sucks

You can't sleep at night. It's difficult to think. You're distressed, distracted and depressed, but you cannot explain it. You can't explain the anger, the insecurity, it's just not rational. Intuitively you feel that something is wrong, but real masculine men aren't allowed to trust their feelings. If it's not a concrete fact or logic, it's not real. It's difficult to tell if you are overcompensating or under compensating in your behavior. This strenuous task of holding the secret makes your life miserable. You are frustrated, confused, frightened and even ashamed although it's really not your fault. You blame yourself for what happened years ago. Living and protecting the secret makes you feel like you have missed out on life. You were not able to live the life that you intended. You're not sure how, why, or when it happened, but there's an inkling in your psyche, soul that something did happen. How has it affected your life? Perhaps you would be a different person if this did not occur. Intimacy with others is a struggle and sexual intimacy with your wife lacks connection. Maybe you inadvertently suppressed the memories because you could not determine if you wanted the abuse to happen. Did you deserve it? Why did the perpetrator pick you? What vibes or signals were being broadcasted from your person that deemed you prey? Did the abuse seem pleasurable or was there any arousal? Why didn't you fight back, scream, and yell? Why didn't you tell your parents or the authorities what happened? Your mind is exploding with questions and unresolved feelings that seem to have no definite answers. You finally start to realize the sexual abuse which you minimized has affected you.

Where to Turn

Now that you waited until adulthood to disclose the secret what will others think? There is an anger deep within that consumes and no one can understand. All your life you have heard the words "Christians aren't supposed to be angry", but no one can tell you what you're supposed to do. You feel less than a man and embarrassed to share the secret with anyone. You are living a lie. You believe that you cannot be the person you desire to be. Church is supposed to be a safe place, but you know it's a lie. They say it's a place of love, acceptance and being your brother's keeper; a place where the love of Jesus conquers all, except the way Christians react to this taboo subject. You have seen the reality of condemnation, ridicule and ostracizing expressed to those men who sought help. Disclosing this secret is worse than death. You are labeled. Yeah, even the pastor, elders and church counselor feel inadequate in addressing your situation. Although such information should be held in privacy, often there are leaks. You contemplate traveling outside your faith for what has been termed secular professional help; however it's difficult to explain faith to someone who does not embrace it. At church, if you disclose, parents will not trust you. Male colleagues socially reject you. It's frustrating. Why are men discriminated against in this arena? Refuge and help are offered to women, but not readily to men. You have nowhere to turn but inward toward isolation. Not because you perpetrated any crime although treated like a criminal, but because you are guilty of being a male victim of childhood sexual abuse. Welcome to a world experienced by millions of male survivors sitting in the church pews on Sunday.

Wow! What a pessimistic view for a Christian, right? Wrong. It is the reality of male survivors of faith who must keep silent so that faith communities can ignore addressing this problem. I have been told that this issue does not readily exist among men of faith. It only exists in the secular world filled the with Sandusky Penn State and Syracuse sport scandals. Tell that to the numerous men who call me in the middle of night freaked and spooked by nightmares and vivid flashbacks of being violated or those who attend the workshops because the wife is leaving with the kids if he doesn't figure out the origins for the outbursts of anger he experiences trying to deal with the abuse. Explain that to the man so terrified by the possible ramifications of disclosing his secret of sexual abuse to his family and loved ones that he jumps from a moving car at 60mph. That's the reality we ignore.

Let's Get Personal

I was the martial arts tiger, rough and tough. I had won regional combat tournaments. When the convenience store was attacked the assailant didn't have a prayer. If the robber had planned to escape with the stolen goods, he had to go through me. I disarmed him and smashed him into the wall. I was steel on the outside but no martial arts training had prepared me for the battle of facing the aftermath of childhood sexual abuse in my adult life.

Twenty years passed since the sexual abuse incidents. My roommate and I cruised to the theater to watch a movie. From the title and reviews of the movie, it seemed like a good murder mystery. That is, until they showed the victim being sexually abused, tortured, and murdered. I can't fully express the powerful emotions and thoughts triggered by the film. My mind flashed with images that had been buried for decades. I couldn't stop them. I saw faces and people. I re-experienced the violations, betrayals, sexual abuse, and torture. Horror flooded my mind. We left the theater, but the avalanche had been triggered. I cried, trembled, agonized, sobbed, and experienced uncontrollable outbursts, rage, anger, fear, doubt, and hopelessness in the weeks to follow. I felt isolated and alone. I experienced depression and began a suicide death march. I reached out in desperation to those I believed would help give comfort and compassion, but I found rejection, embarrassment and shame. A devoted Christian contemplating suicide resonated with tones of blasphemous condemnation. It's difficult to remember the details, but my death march began. The next 36-72 hours became a blur. I walked for hours in a mind altered state of pain, a dark fog. I have no recollection and cannot recount how I ended up at my friend's door miles away with no car; perhaps subconsciously I wanted to say-goodbye. This pain had to end.

Numerous men are tortured by the secret of such abuse. Men are not allowed to be victims of sexual crimes especially in Christian circles. It's a triple whammy! We are forced into silence and isolation. We would rather suffer with unresolved hurt and unfilled lives and dysfunctional behavior than disclose and be labeled as unmanly or gay by our Christian colleagues who may not have the ability to comprehend. For some men the years of secrecy and pain have manifested into addictions, feelings of inadequacies and other destructive behaviors that have destroyed their marriages, families and relationships. The struggle to break this pattern is often useless because the past abuse which impacted our development is ignored. If you are tired of the hurt, the confusion, or embarrassment in dealing with your abuse, then I suggest using this book as part of your recovering toolbox. It's time for a reboot.

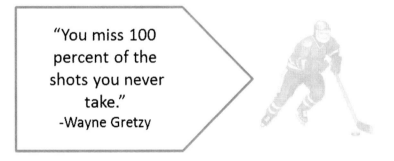

"You miss 100 percent of the shots you never take."
-Wayne Gretzy

Mixing Spiritual and Psychological?

Why spiritual and psychological? Honestly, I believe the two disciplines often collaborate with each other. The word psychology derives its origin from the word "psyche" which means soul. Of course, the Bible ultimately deals with the heart and soul of man. It's definitely a great resource when applied appropriately. Psychology often provides some practical applications for dealing with certain issues, while biblical principles can help guide our direction and provide a constant source of hope. I have encountered survivor programs based on psychology which have delivered some great outcomes. Therefore it is not practical to discredit all components in this field simply because one may not agree with some of its tenets. However those desiring their faith to be an integral part of the healing path can utilize both. It was the spiritual truth of Christ manifested in a friend that saved me from the dark abyss of despair and suicide. It is the strategies and techniques of psychology that have offered pragmatic tools for coping and recovery. Is this integration for every male survivor's experience? No. I encounter survivors who suffered ritualistic abuse at the hands of religious leaders claiming to be follower of God. In such instance a person's faith maybe shattered and destroyed and no affiliation with anything considered spiritual or faith-based is desired. However some still manage to hold remnants of their faith. It's for those survivors that desire integration of the two. It helped my situation as I needed to know that I had intrinsic value outside of myself. Therefore God was part of the key for me and no matter how horrible it seemed He reminded me of my value. This value is granted to you also by the God who created you in His image (Genesis 1:25-27). Nothing can ever change that truth. This was a belief that helped to transverse the pain and rejection I often experienced. During perhaps the most painful and vulnerable time in Jesus' life, the Garden of Gethsemane, He exemplified three key components that we can use also. We want men dealing with CSA to thrive not just survive. The mission is to continue helping other men by raising awareness, conducting workshops to help them find their voice. That's the reason the two disciplines can work well together.

Do you ever feel like this picture? Trapped, helpless and broken! When dealing with the issues of childhood sexual abuse feeling like this is not unusual. This is often how our life looks when attempting to tackle a difficult problem alone. You know, the manly way, "I can do it myself! I don't need help!" I also have encountered times when feeling the false shame or hurt of the sexual abuse prompted me to take this route. It wasn't until I gave credence and validity to Proverbs 18:1 "Whoever isolates himself seeks his own desire; he rages against all sound wisdom" that my healing started to sprout wings. Each time I have an opportunity to conduct a workshop or support group, and share strategies, principles and stories. I grow and heal. I simply want to encourage you not to isolate yourself. Get serious about the desire to heal from the CSA or any issue and take the next step.

Pen Action: Take some time to journal what you are experiencing right now.

Chapter Two
Hard Questions

The value that you have within yourself first comes from without. Value is always assigned from an outside source. You can destroy that value by living life that is not authentic to that value or allowing others to devalue you.

Is this Reality?

The 2012 Syracuse, Penn State Jerry Sandusky scandal has generated a little more attention to the subject of male childhood sexual abuse in our society. Perhaps one of the reasons it has captured our attention revolves around tarnishing one of America's favorite past times, sports. Our own sayings *"as American as baseball and apple pie"* demonstrates the relevance sports play in our American culture as being considered normal. (I often find when conducting workshops that this mentality of masculinity being associated with sports is often used as pseudo reparative treatment by parents hoping to eradicate the perceived threats the sexual abuse has towards the child's gender. We will discuss more at length later.)

The American Dream has been a nightmare for male survivors for years. Let's view two families. In house number one we have a portrait of a loving father and mother raising two or three children in a comfortable home. Dad works for a corporate giant or medium-sized business, while Mom works at home and volunteers a few hours a week at the local hospital. The children attend school and are involved in sports, piano lessons, or other extracurricular activities. Home is a place where the children experience a protected environment that is supportive, comforting, and pleasant, but there exist a secret that Dad possesess that will change the coarse of this family in the next five months. On this same block of our idyllic surroundings lives another family. From outer appearances we see a loving, family. Like any family, they have problems, but nothing that would seem out of the ordinary. John works very hard at two jobs making sure his family enjoys the basic needs and a few comforts, while Martha spends her time raising the kids during the day, and working a part-time job in the evening to help keep financial obligations afloat. The kids are normal. They experience a little sibling rivalry between them. They play X-box, watch American Idol, and do school work. Let's extrapolate these two families to represent typical families in our society. Research conservatively reports that in our homes 1 in 6 boys are sexually abused. A research study, *Long-term Consequences of Childhood Sexual Abuse By Gender of Victim*, in the American Journal of Preventive Medicine, approximates that one of six boys is sexually abused. This number is assumed quite conservative due to unreported cases. The number is believed to be greater but let's use the reported numbers. If we give that ratio a pictorial representation, it amounts to 18 million boys/men have experienced some type of sexual abuse. With organizations like Man Boy Love Association, child pornography rings, and human sex trafficking outfits the actual incidents are believed to be worse. For each child victim, innocence has been stolen and trust violated. Unimaginable changes and struggles will require years of painful unraveling.

Are Believers Immune?

Christians, people of faith, believers are not immune. We get flat tires, mosquito bites, cancer and can be sexually abused just like everyone else. However, in the faith communities we associate the sexual abuse of boys as a Catholic problem because of the scandals reported in the news. It's not acknowledged as an issue experienced in other denominations like Evangelicals, Baptists, Assemblies of God, Pentecostals, Methodist, Lutheran, United Reform, United African Methodist, Community church, Orthodox, Mennonite, Berean, Christian congregational, Church of Christ, Foursquare, Covenant, LDS, Jehovah Witness, Apostolic, Wesleyan, Moravian, Presbyterian and the list continues. In denial, we keep our heads hidden in the sand hoping the issue will disappear. We placate our conscious by not investigating or researching the issue and how it pertains to the congregations we attend. How real is this in Christian circles?

Jim called me at 2 am from Rhode Island freaked out. His voice cracked as he attempted to articulate the inward war he fought. "My wife is threatening to leave with the kids if I don't get help." He seemed reluctant to divulge. "I have so much anger and fear and I can't make it go away. My pastor tells me to pray and read my bible more for the anger issue. I think he's afraid to talk about the sexual abuse with me. I tried opening up to a few friends at church. However, they have secretly labeled me as emasculated and probably gay. The teenage class has been reassigned to someone else. Gossip in the pews is that people who were abused will abuse others. That's not even an issue for me. How can they think that? People are avoiding me like a leper. I get suspicious glares when holding my own kids. This is such a backwards thinking group. Of course I'm angry and frustrated. I'm trying to ask and seek help and I'm being treated like a criminal because of what someone else did to me." Multiply Jim's frustration with his faith community and we start to assess a prevalent problem in churches across the nation. Yes, it is real! It's time to educate ourselves so we can help others instead of becoming a hindrance to healing growth.

Was I Abused?

Often I encounter victims of CSA who believe their lives are normal and unaffected by the sexual abuse. From his perspective not much is wrong, but from a veteran's look you can surmise it's beyond his control. He is not convinced that talking about the experience or how it might partly influence his problems today. By isolating himself and suppressing the pain inside he tries not to think or feel. Ironically, he feels great anger, rage, sadness and shame, but he will never express these feelings because it's not encouraged. It's not safe. He has never learned to deal with intense emotions, at least in a conducive manner. He copes in the way that he is expected to by controlling and manipulating his environment turning the rage outward and hurting others in his life by silently clinging to the secret of his abuse.

Only in the past few years have therapists and counselors even addressed or tried to understand male victims of sexual abuse. As men it has been a great challenge attempting to overcome the social pressures and norms placed on men to be mentally and emotionally unaffected by the abuse. To verbally or emotionally express our weakness and vulnerabilities is often frowned on. (Sorry Ms. Snively, I ended with a preposition) Because of this socialization we have been trained to disregard and ignore inklings or impressions that point to the unwanted sexual abuse.

Terry shares

Terry sat behind the controls at the radio station. He seemed perplexed during the radio show. After the show I reorganized my notes and placed them in the computer bag. I always made a point of dropping by after the show to thank the engineers. Terry grabbed my arm. "Do you have a moment? I would like to ask you a question."

I nodded and we walked into the sound proof room. "I really appreciate your ministry. I think that I'm a statistic, 1 in 6, but I'm not sure." We sat and Terry leaned forward almost whispering. "This is something that has always bothered me. I remember as a kid my Dad taking me to the doctor's appointment. Umm…well I think the doctor fondled me and did other things as if giving me a physical exam. This happened repeatedly. I felt nausea in my stomach. I was afraid. I didn't know if that's what doctors did for exams. One day father asked me what was going on. I simply told him. He became angry at me and told me to never do that again. We never went back to see the doctor again. My mother took me to her female doctor and I experienced a similar incident. It happened once. We never saw that doctor again. My dad never said anything else, but he has treated me different after that day. My mom never talks about it. I know this sounds crazy, but was I sexually abused? What made them want to do that to me? Was I projecting some type of vibes that I wanted this? With my father's reaction to what occurred, I have always had the notion that something was wrong with me."

When portraying male victims of sexual abuse we have been led to envision unmanly, effeminate adults whose life is a total dysfunctional mess. We have been falsely trained by media, rumors and ignorance to search for illusions. When in reality, many victims are high-functioning respected individuals and productive citizens. This does not mean they are minimally hurt or impacted compared to others who may visibly display some of the negative effects associated with the abuse. Many men confronting the possibility of acknowledging the sexual abuse speak of doubting their memories, especially if they are abstract and vague. We have been socialized to think; "just the facts" and anything that deviates from that standard, like a feeling, inkling or intuitive notion are to be disregarded. We must conclusively prove that we were sexually abused. In the hopes of not being abused, or accusing a family member of betrayal and neglect, we would rather be labeled as a bit crazy or assume the abuse as our fault and being "bad". Perhaps the view or concept to consider is not specific details, but imprints of boundary violations if the memory is unclear. In the workshops sometimes men will express knowing that "something" happened, but unable to produce a vivid detailed memory. From a psychological perspective, it is important to acknowledge that sexual abuse, whether physical or emotional is considered a form of invasion. It is not always necessary to focus solely on the specific act. It is up to us to address that sense of violation and betrayal as it manifests in our lives today. .

How Do I Define Abuse?

Abuse itself can be defined as excessive and wrongful misuse of a person or thing. There are different types of abuse: physical and sexual abuse, drug abuse, verbal abuse, or emotional abuse. I have found defining sexual abuse within the realm of male victimization is complicated. The definition of sexual abuse may vary especially from a psychological or legal perspective. We often identify two main categories that sexual abuse can fall into contact and noncontact. Contact involves behaviors such as sexual stimulation, arousal, and penetration whether successful or attempted, touching, forced enemas, coercion of bestiality, masturbation, fondling, intercourse, child prostitution and the list continues. Noncontact might involve behaviors like sexual acts in front of a child, sexualized talk, voyeurism, child pornography, encouraging child to be sexual with others, deriving sexual pleasure from spanking. Even within these definitions there exist subtle undertones like seduction that may be considered abusive although not explicit in nature. (It's not easy naming these behaviors, but it's necessary for men to start understanding how their experience may have involved abuse, although not commonly perceived as abuse.)

Any Signs I May Have Been Abused?

Are there any scars? Maybe there are not physical scars, but are there scars in the form of abnormal behaviors? This list is not inclusive of everything possible scenario but offers some common behavior patterns to consider if you are suspicious of the possibility. Men were surveyed at the workshop concerning behavior patterns they experienced and felt were related. (Realize that sexual abuse many not be the only reason for these exhibited behaviors and attitudes.)

- Explosive temper, anger
- Drinking problem
- Always feeling hopeless
- Drug, substance abuse
- Low esteem, poor self-image
- Enjoys being isolated, alone, withdrawn
- Sexual addiction
- Always feeling let down or betrayed by others
- Allows himself to be bullied or is the bully
- Thinks Everyone has an ulterior motive

- Difficulties loving his children, especially sons
- Difficulty being intimate with others, that's not sexual
- Afraid of being close in proximity to other men
- Equates sex to love
- Compulsive behavior in many things (work, eating, sex)
- Always critical of himself and others
- Extreme fear of homosexuality
- Mistrusts practically everyone
- Insecure about masculinity
- Issues of fidelity, must prove I'm okay and normal
- Violent with spouse
- Same-sex attraction
- Dreams of being abused, smothered

Emotional Abuse

How powerful is emotional abuse or manipulation? Perpetrators often use verbal or emotional abuse to undermine a child's perceptions to manipulate him. This is achieved by isolating the child from the truth, and from contact with others. This allows the abuser to exercise control over the child. The perpetrator creates confusion in the child, and causes both emotional pain and mental grief. The perpetrator then prepares to be the rescuer. A strong component of child sexual abuse and molestation therefore involves emotional abuse. This systematic tearing down of the child seriously interferes with the child's development. This emotional abuse is probably the least understood but most prevalent part of sexual abuse. It assaults the child's understanding and concept of self. It makes the child feel unworthy of love and affection.

Even if you feel that your sexual abuse wasn't physically damaging or painful, emotional abuse can deprive you of basic nurturing. This might fostered insecurity, anxiety, and low self-esteem. One of the common stories men have shared with me is the emotional abuse and abandonment by loved ones that often follows the abuse. We live in a world where daycare, iPods, organized sports, and extracurricular activities replace quality family time. Strong emotional bonds are not always formed between child and parent. This sets the child up to have those needs fulfilled elsewhere. This creates the perfect environment for certain types of abuse, especially sexual abuse, to take place. Years later, this part of the abuse is often most difficult for men to admit and overcome. Emotional abuse comes in different forms. I have encountered abuse ranging from verbal abuse, inappropriate sexual talk, neglect, physical violence, child pornography, psychological mind games, abandonment, and rape. Abuse to children manifests in many ways.

Rejection: The adult often rejects the child. I have encountered numerous men who were told they were worthless or unwanted, or would never amount to anything. In some cases, all the family's problems are projected onto the helpless child for acknowledging or bringing up the abuse.

Ignoring: The adult shows no interest in displaying affection or attachment towards the child. The adults are physically there, but emotionally absent. One of the most neglected expressions of affection for men is the safe, legitimate physical contact by a respected male figure. One workshop participant stated, "I wished my father would have just told me he loved me." Another said, "My father never hugged me. I felt like a leper." These are common expressions often expressed as men start opening up.

Terrorizing: The adult singles out the child to punish, criticize or hurt him. The child becomes the object of ridicule, especially if he displays normal emotions. In sexual abuse, the child can be threatened with death, abandonment, or torture.

Isolation: The adult does not allow the child to engage in activities with his peers. She keeps the child locked in his room, and he is not allowed to participate in extracurricular activities. This builds a false sense of dependency on the adult and limits interaction with others. He has no social skills in relating to his peers.

Corrupting: The adult permits the child to use drugs, pornographic materials, or witness criminal activity, such as assault, prostitution, or theft. Such corruption eventually allows the abuser to commit the treacherous act with the child, who perceives it as normal.

One of the great challenges for men is defining and admitting the sexual abuse. No matter how we define sexual abuse whether using psychological or legal terms the reluctance of disclosure by male survivors will partially depend on his definition or view. For example, if the survivor experiences fondling by the perpetrator and believes this action is less impactful than penetration, he may consider it non-abusive or unimportant to disclose. What man wants to admit that a loved one, friend, or stranger he trusted sexually violated him? It may be difficult to accept or use this word abuse. However in working through the issue it's beneficial to consider using this term. Another word that works more on relational level that describes the abuse is betrayal. As a child you were betrayed. I'm defining the betrayal as those who exploited your trust, dependency and need for protection and love in order to fulfill their own selfish desires. Sexual abuse which can involve physical, psychological and emotional components wounds the soul and spirit of the child, who will grow into adulthood.

Read: Exodus 15:22-26

Do you ever feel like the children of Israel? Have the bitter experiences of life caused you to murmur or forget God? God does not hinder the struggles, hurts, and conflicts of life. Yet He offers to be there as we work through the painful experiences. He offers to heal our ailments. While healing us, He can use us to help others.

Pen Action: Take the time to journal the following questions.

- Name any of the emotional abuses listed above that you experienced

- Name other that may not be included on the list

- How do you observe any of these affecting your life today?

- Do you find yourself displaying these same types of emotional abuses towards your own children, spouse or in other relationships?

- In your own words, define your abuse.

Prayer:

Lord, please help me to continue to address grief and pain. The abuse hurts me in ways that I cannot totally understand, but I feel and see it affecting my life. Grant me the courage at this time to grow stronger and not lose heart. Help me to renounce any pride and to open my heart for your healing.

Ryan's Story

Getting close to a person was always difficult. I was always afraid the person would never reciprocate or give back. I gave everything I had. I was a yes-man, a pleaser. My father had a temper and always had to be pleased; everything had to be his way or he became angry. You didn't want to upset him. He was very intimidating, strict, and unaffectionate. I never told my parents about the man who was abusing me. He was a friend of the family. He was married with kids of his own. He also had a slight temper. If I didn't perform right, he would become upset and tell me I was failing him. Being a failure seemed more painful than the actual abuse. I didn't want to fail him because he supplied the only form of affection that made me feel loved. I kept trying to please him as it was the quickest way for the abuse to be finished. The abuse continued several years into my adolescent years. Even today, I'm still a yes-man, often to my detriment. I still want to be loved.

Ryan's short story illustrates how abuse can have long term effects. He is stuck. He finally took action to change the tragic aftermath caused by the abuse when he attended the workshop. Like others, he convinced himself of the lie that time heals all wounds. Ryan finally realized the personal responsibility for taking action to heal and his world opened up. He learned how to address not only the issues of the abuse, but also the strained relationship he experienced with his father. Perhaps you are uncovering more refuse dumped in your personal emotional, spiritual and psychological backyard by the perpetrator and it's not fun cleaning it up. However clean it up you must, because no one can help you remove this trash from your yard until you decide, "It's got to go!"

That's Not My Job
(by: Author Unknown, Source Unknown)

This is a story about four people: Everybody, Somebody, Anybody and Nobody. There was an important job to be done and Everybody was sure that Somebody would do it. Anybody could have done it but Nobody did it. Somebody got angry about that, because it was Everybody's job. Everybody thought Anybody could do it, but Nobody realized that Everybody wouldn't do it. It ended up that Everybody blamed Somebody when Nobody did what Anybody should have done.

> **Truths and Promises**
>
> Those who sow in tears shall reap with joyful shouting. He whogoes to and fro weeping, carrying his bag of seed, shall indeed come again with a shout of joy, bringing his sheaves with him. *Psalm 126: 5-6*
>
> Therefore you too have grief now; but I will see you again, and your heart will rejoice, and no one will tak your joy away from you. *John 16:22e*

What Forms of Sexual Abuse?

It's difficult to stomach discussing childhood sexual abuse. Our society tends to dampen the effects of certain crimes by using politically correct language that softens the tone. For example, have you ever really thought about the term child molester? That's right up there with harassment. Molest means to bother. In other words, someone is bothering the child. I don't think so! Sexual violation is often used to fulfill an underlying motive often for control and power. The abuser may have been prompted by insecurities, the exhilaration of exercising power over another–which is bullying--or to allay aggressions within. The touch violation or physical aspect is not always the most harmful portion. In some abuse situations no physical contact is involved. Examples of this are photographing child pornography, or coercing the boy to masturbate. Regardless, the intent and meaning behind the actions are deceitfully portrayed as acts of love. Whether blatant or inconspicuous, sexual abuse to any child may be manifested in various forms:

- Fondling the child
- Sexualized language
- Making the child view pornography
- Exposing of genitals for gratification
- Performing sexual acts in front of the child,
- Voyeurism of a teenage boy or girl
- Bestiality
- Child prostitution
- Bribes
- Torture
- Threats to coerce child into sexual acts.

Why Was I So Naive?

This feeling and thought are so common. At the workshops at least 75% of the participants struggle with this question. Many blame themselves for what happened. I believe it's important to understand the concept and world of grooming if we are ever to take the sexual abuse bull by the horns and reclaim our lives. Let's dive in and undertand a bit more about grooming.

- Gain trust
- Break down defenses
- Manipulate to perform the wanted sexual acts

Yes, it seems like a formula. It may not fit every single situation and scenario but definitely serves as the basis for how pretrators often groom their victims. If the prepertator has to first go through the child's parent or caretaker, he/she will employ the same techniques to access the child. Such techniques increases the opportunities to access the victim and decrease the chances of being discovered. The process starts when the predator selects or aims at this target. In our situation young boys. Often the perpetrator will visit places where the victim is likely to be found: parks, playgrounds, backyards, shopping malls, schools, sports events, churches. Many of the guys often report that their perpetrators where similar to the Sandusky case where and individual works with as a volunteer sports organization or charity that caters to children. Predators who must first get past adults often strike up relationships with parents. The number one reported target is children of single parents. Any child can be targeted, however predators often select children who appear vulnerable. Children who are unpopular, feel unloved, unimportant, lack confidence, low self-esteem, spend time alone or dealing with family problems like a divorce are prime targets.

There different ways in which the perpetrator recruits his victims. Force, charm, coercion, threats, and seduction are a few. Gifts , treats or other things are given as tokens of friendship to help breakdown the defensive walls. Teenagers often are offered drugs or alcohol to win them over. The psychological gift often used is offering the sympathetic understanding ear when no one else, whom the child trusts, will listen. They will seek isolate others from the mental picture, " You can trust me. I respect you. I care for you more than anybody esle. I love you. "

It is often at this point the prepetrator introduces secrecy into the process. It is this bond of secrecy that can wreak havoc our entire lives when left buried. As adult men we are still caught in the grooming techniques of the perpetrator. „"Don't tell your friends or family because they will not understand. If you tell what happened, they will hate you or blame you. Or I'll kill you. People will think you are weird." After the emotion bond has been forged through this process, and the walls broken down often the physical contact begins. Often this process slowly increases the acceptance of touch. Non-sexual touch is used to desensitize the child so that later more overt sexual touching is possible.

- Trust/Favoritism
- Isolation/Secrecy
- Desensitization
- Sexual Abuse

You are not to blame – no child can ever hold responsibility for their sexual abuse nor take the responsibility for the actions of an adult.

Myths about Abusers

Amazing myths surround the perpetrators of childhood sexual abuse to boys. We have allowed media and popular legend to thwart our minds, to look for the dirty old man living in the red light district in the basement of some apartment or shack. In so doing, we hurt our children. We need to watch for the signs in front of us. One phrase always seems to come up when the perpetrator is discovered: "He/She seemed like a normal person. He/She was kind, friendly, and never hurt anyone." The facts are:

- Over 70% of perpetrators are related or close in familiarity to the child.
- Most sexual abuse involves repeated offenses.
- Children are often bribed, coerced or threatened into sexual abuse situations.
- Heterosexual men, usually married, are the most prevalent perpetrators.
- A woman sexually manipulating a boy is still abuse.

If you believe this behavior is more prevalent among those of poor socio-economic backgrounds, please stop believing the myth. It spans across race, geography, ethnic class and religion. Boys are victimized across the nation. It's a sad picture. It's difficult to find more data and accurate facts on sexual abuse because there is no standardized or accepted definition of sexual abuse to compare the studies.

Pen Action: Check if any of these were part of your unwanted sexual abuse experience. This is designed to help you realize that sexual abuse doesn't have to be necessarily violent in nature. We often think that it should be less impactful if it was not physically torturous. In such cases men frequently attempt to minimize they were abused. This list is not complete, but provides descriptions of some of the common atrocities. Feel free to include others.

__ Adult exposing him/herself for gratification

__ Verbal abuse of sexual nature

__ Caressed while sleeping

__ Forced bestiality

__ Viewing others being sexual abused

__ Child prostitution

__ Emotional abuse of sexual nature

__ Adult sexually touching you

__ Inviting a child to touch adult's sexual organs

__ Photographing child for sexual purposes

__ Purposely undressing in front of you

__ Showing pornographic material to you

__ Teasing a child concerning sexual development

__ Masturbating in front of a child

__ Voyeurism

__ Coercing you to masturbate, or together

__ Constantly bathing a child who can bathe himself

__ Fondling

__ Other

Pen Action: Take some time to journal the following questions.

- Would you consider yourself sexually abused or molested?

- What do you feel/think the word that you chose implies?

- How do you define sexual abuse?

- How difficult is it to think of yourself as having been sexually abused?

- How does your definition of abuse help you to acknowledge/ignore/ or dismiss the impact of being abused by someone or a loved one?

- List the emotions you felt when reading or checking off the abuses on the list.

Prayer:

Lord, addressing this truth is really difficult for me to face and admit. I'm having a difficult time admitting that this really happened to me. It's painful and it hurts to think about it. Those who were supposed to love me used me for their own gratification! I didn't ask for this! But it has happened to me. Please grant me strength and courage to face these issues.

> **Truths and Promsies**
>
> Cast your burden upon the LORD and He will sustain you; He will never allow the righteous to be shaken. *Psalm 55:22*
>
> The LORD's loveing kindnesses indeed never cease, for His compassions never fail. They are new every morning; Great is your faithfulness. "The LORD is my portion," says my souul, "Therefore I have hope in *Lamentations 3:22-24*

> Now may the God of Hope fill you with all joy and peace in believing so that you will aboutnd in hope by the power of the Holy Spirit. *Romans 15:13*

The Bucket

This illustration was shared with me years ago. I modified it for using at the workshop.

This is an illustration of a bucket that is like the overflowing cup, only larger. It is an invisible bucket. Everyone has one. It determines how we feel about ourselves, about others, and how we get along with people. Have you ever experienced a series of very favorable things which made you want to be good to people for a whole week or even just a day? At that time your bucket was full. The bucket can be filled by a lot of things. When a person speaks to you, recognizing you as human, your bucket is filled a little. It is filled more if he calls you by name, especially if he calls you by the name you like. Or if a woman compliments you on something, the level in your bucket rises higher. When ones bucket is full of this emotional support, one can express warmth and friendliness to people. When people have had traumatic experiences, they often have holes in their buckets. When a person has holes, his life cannot be full. The holes must be repaired, sealed and healed. The key is to seal the holes and repair your bucket. As God, friends, and family start filling your bucket, you will start filling other people's buckets. People who hesitate filling the bucket of others have difficulties experiencing happiness, fulfillment, and connection. I hope that by writing this book, I can give and help to fill a small portion of your bucket

 I Learned That...

- It's okay to have feelings. The problems often come from not doing anything to resolve the issues.
- Buried hurt manifests distrust, hurt, anger and sorrow.

- Attempting to run away from my thoughts and hurt are like trying to run away from my shadow. I can't outrun it.
- Hurting people hurt people, perhaps inadvertently as a defensive mechanism. Often I didn't realize that I was hurting others because I couldn't see past my own pain.

Take a Break!

Before you continue, stop! Take a walk. Breathe deeply as you walk. Walk for about 15-20 minutes through a park or forest. Enjoy the natural beauty around you. Think about how blessed you are to be finally working through some of the issues. Take a couple of days, weeks whatever you need, to process your journey up to this point.

Pen Action: Take some time to journal what you are experiencing right now.

Chapter Three
Family Hurts

Revealing the sexual abuse can cause an explosion in a family. Suddenly the family has to look at itself in a different way. It's not fun realizing you are not the happy family you perceived.

Jack Shares

Jack was medium build, quite intelligent and a handsome guy. He reported sexual and physical abuse from his early childhood. His abuse began around age 7. When he attended his grandparents on weekends his grandmother's bathing rituals were excessive with fondling while his dad would threaten to castrate him if he did not perform. Jack was befuddled. He could not comprehend why his grandparent and dad were doing this to him. Being reared in conservative religious family, sex was always touted as being bad, evil and people who engaged in sex were hell bound. Of course he surmised himself as bad, evil and headed toward hell. He assumed his sexual orientation was gay because he and his father were the same gender. In his college fraternity initiation he was humiliated and hazed and forced to fellatio some of his frat brothers. As a kid his only coping mechanisms were running away, withdrawing inward, and fantasying about living with the normal family down the street. At age 40, he's attempting to unravel his co-dependent nature, stay sober and stop using promiscuity as a badge to prove he's not gay. He has low self-respect and esteem, and he questions the worth of his Christian beliefs.

Read: 2 Samuel 13:1-21

Perhaps one of most tragic forms of sexual abuse is incest. The parent, sibling, relative, or close family friend who the child trusts to protect him becomes the violator. This can be one of worst betrayals for you or as a male survivor to experience. Who could you have turned to for security, comfort, and understanding? When we use the word "family" the person doesn't necessarily have to be a blood relative. It may be a friend who's considered an extended part of the family. The person could be a priest, a scout leader, coach, and teacher--any person who holds trusted familial characteristics. To a child, family is considered the safe zone, and the people within this circle are believed to be trustworthy. Strangers are portrayed as outsiders and unsafe. Therefore, when a child is sexually abused by a member of the family, everything he has known about familial trust, structure and protection has been destroyed. This often creates confusion, pain, and leaves emotional scaring.

Survivors report that as boys the familial abuse sometimes started out as horseplay, tickling, roughhousing and wrestling by a loved adult. Unfortunately, this often serves as one of the only flashbacks or memories of love and positive interaction. Often the horseplay morphed into sexual abuse and undetectable by the child until it happened. Suddenly the child is baffled attempting to understand what is occurring and why this family member whom he admires enjoys hurting him. As the child struggles to determine if this abusive behavior is right, wrong or a mistake a litany of future negative effects have been set in motion. Such atrocities cannot happen in Christian homes in our families. If we believe that we have forgotten the biblical truth and reality of fallen man and his propensity to fall short of God's standard. Yes it does happen.

Tim Shares

Uncle Steve came to live with us during his divorce. He was a cool guy. He was very masculine and had time for me, not like my father, who spent time with me only when he disciplined me. Uncle Steve often teased me about girls, so I felt comfortable and trusted him. When I tried to talk with Dad about girls, and the birds and bees, he told me to look it up in the dictionary. Uncle Steve was an avid fisherman and we often headed up to the lake. He bought me anything I needed for the trip: bait, snacks, or lures, anything I wanted.

Today, I understand this was a part of the grooming process. Yet, even today it's difficult to think of him as a criminal. A portion of the child in me clings to the loving parts of him. As we walked and talked, he always put his hand on my shoulder. He was my good friend.

We had been fishing on the lake for years, but on this particular adventure something was different. As we sat and fished on the bank, he reached across me for a Coke, and he accidently spilt it on my pants. As he tried to wipe the soda out of my lap, things started happening to my body. He said it was okay and natural and nothing to be embarrassed about. That was how it began. Before I knew it, he was doing things to me I didn't understand. It felt strange and exciting at the same time. For years, I have struggled trying to understand my inability to speak up, to do something. Did he really hurt me? It has taken years, but I finally have been able to admit that what he did was sexual abuse. Yet, inside of me there is a small question, "If it felt even a little pleasurable, what does that say about me?" People will not understand when I try to explain this ambivalence. I will be labeled not only as unmasculine, but gay. That's a death sentence in my religious circle. I will be treated different because someone betrayed me and I disclosed that betrayal."

How Has It Shaped Your View?

Hopefully our parents expressed love that resulted in a bond of trust. Our dependence on adults forged opportunities for us to learn about relationships. Hopefully our parents or guardians provided for us. We learned behaviors based on those relationship. As we continued to grow, our relationships with teachers, relatives, and close family was based on parental bonding. As kids, we could not articulate this relationship of trust, nor explain what it meant, but we could **feel** it. It's amazingly interesting the perception and feeling we had before learning the facts and developing our logical reasoning. We were intuitive. As children--if we grow in a loving and trusting environment--we learn to build confidence, support, strength and security into our world. All future relationships and behaviors towards others will be based on the trust established by the loving parents or guardians. Perhaps an easier way to explain is with this scripture:

> Trust in the Lord with all your heart and do not lean on your own understanding in all your ways acknowledge Him, And He will make your paths straight.
> Proverbs 3:5-6

As God's children, we are instructed to place our trust in God, our Father. That trust is based on faith and the evidence of His providential care. Therefore, by relying on Him we know allow God to direct our paths. I believe as children we experience this principle. Based on the child's experience with those in his immediate circle, he will trust and follow intuitively. Within this context he will also learn valuable boundaries, limitations of relationships, and which individuals to trust. These formative years will build and shape his world view.

A child cannot arrange his life as he pleases and must trust out of necessity. He believes that in general people are good based on his experiences. His protectors love, like his parents. He bestows trust to those in authority who seem to have good, loving, and honorable qualities, like Mom and Dad. Sexual abuse undermines that foundation of the child's world. This traumatic experience shatters his world and he instinctively creates defensive mechanisms to dismantle this new reality. Therefore a parent, a relative or friend who acts as the perpetrator confuses the child by distorting what he understands as truth. The perpetrator does not have the child's interest at heart. This confronts him with the new reality that sexual gratification trumps love. Who will protect the child now? It's a difficult reality to grasp. We all want to believe that our parents, family, friends, loved ones did the best for us as children. As adults, we may not totally agree with every parenting method, but in general we believe our parents did their best raise us in a godly way with love. This treachery of incestuous sexual abuse destroys that foundational love. This lie fosters emotional betrayal and forges insecurity. We gasp in horror and disbelief that such events are part of our world, but even more so in Christian homes.   Sexual abuse and incest existed in biblical times. I always thought this an interesting point. God has no problem mentioning sexual abuse as the reality of a fallen world, yet in our religious communities we dare not utter its existence.

> "Then Amnon said to Tamar, "Bring the food into the bedroom, that I may eat from your hand." So Tamar took the cakes which she had made and brought them into the bedroom to her brother Amnon. When she brought them to him to eat, he took hold of her and said to her, "Come, lie with me, my sister."   But she answered him, "No, my brother, do not violate me, for such a thing is not done in Israel; do not do this disgraceful thing! "As for me, where could I get rid of my reproach? And as for you, you will be like one of the fools in Israel. Now therefore, please speak to the king, for he will not withhold me from you." However, he would not listen to her; since he was stronger than she, he violated her and lay with her Then Amnon hated her with a very great hatred; for the hatred with which he hated her was greater than the love with which he had loved her. And Amnon said to her, "Get up, go away!" 2 Samuel 13:10-15

Scared Boys Terrified Men|

Pen Action: Take some time to journal the following questions.

In the questions below, rewrite the numbered statements that are your realities. These are truths about what has happened to you that you must face and admit. Then read the statements out loud if you are able. This exercise has helped me and others face the truth, and supply more courage to open up. It might take time, so be patient. If you are not ready, come back to it later. Write more in a journal if you need to express your feelings on paper.

- I was sexually abused as a child. My sexual abuse involved…

- The sexual act that was committed against me was wrong…

- It was ………… to commit this act of betrayal against me!

Prayer:

God, the pain I am experiencing right now feels overwhelming. You promised in your word that you will not allow us to bear more than we can handle. I feel alone and isolated. It's difficult to focus and concentrate on this promise being real for me. Forgive me for my doubt and impatience. I am not certain I can endure. There is a lot buried within my soul. It's a challenge to be open and be vulnerable. I am afraid that people will judge and condemn and place hurtful labels and stigmas on me, making it even worse. Help me to reach out and find support resources that are loving and kind like You.

He said, "O man of high esteem, do not be afraid. Peace be with you; take courage and be courageous!" Now as soon as he spoke to me, I received strength and said, "May my lord speak, for you have strengthened me." Daniel 10:19

A Friend...

by: Author Unknown,
(A)ccepts you as you are
(B)elieves in "you"
(C)alls you just to say "HI"

(D)oesn't give up on you
(E)nvisions the whole of you
(F)orgives your mistakes
(G)ives unconditionally
(H)elps you
(I)nvites you over
(J)ust to "be" with you
(K)eeps you close at heart
(L)oves you for who you are
(M)akes a difference in your life
(N)ever blindly condemns
(O)ffers support
(P)icks you up
(Q)uiets your fears
(R)aises your spirits
(S)ays nice things about you
(T)ells you the truth when you need to hear it
(U)nderstands you
(V)alues you
(W)alks beside you
(X)-plains thing you don't understand
(Y)ells when you won't listen
(Z)aps you back to reality

In building your circle of help find a friend for each of these on the list. Can you imagine a support group of 26 people?

Truths and Promises

He gives strength to the weary and to him who lacks might. He increases power. Though youths grow weary and tired, and vigorous young men stumble badly, yet those who wait for the Lord wiill gain new strength; they will mount up with wings as eagles, they will run and not get tired, they will walk and not become weary. *Isaiah 40:29-31*

We are afflicted in every way, but not crushed; perplexed, but not despairing; persecuted, but not forsaken; struck down but not destroyed; Therefore we do not lose heart, but though our outer man is decaying, yet our inner man is being renewed day by day. For momentary, light affliction is producing for us an eternal weight of glory far beyond all comparison, while we look not at things which are seen, but at things which are not seen; for the things which are seen are temporal, but the things which are not seen are eternal. *2 Corinthians 4:8-9, 16-18*

Read: 1 Corinthians 13: 4-13

Pen Action: Read and journal

- You may have considered the sexual abuse as loving. Journal about these words found in this passage "Love…does not insist on its own way".

- Does the abusive experience fit into this love category?

- How was your perpetrator/abuser "seeking his/her own" interests?

- How was the abuse in your best interest?

- As a victim of sexual abuse, List ways you might possibly minimize the traumatic experience.

- What is the truth about your specific abuse?

- How do you see the virtues of faith, hope, and love helping you through this healing process?

- Faith is based on evidence, so write down the evidence you have that God does/does not love you.

- Hope is based on two components "desire and expectation". Write about an expectation and desire you want to achieve as you overcome and heal from sexual abuse. Be specific! For example, "My expectation and desire is to heal from the hurt and pain, and be able to build a better relationship with my spouse."

- Read the scripture again concerning love. List several people that you know who love you.

Truths and Promises

"The steadfast of mind You will keep in perfect peace, Because he trusts in You." Trust in the Lord forever, For in GOD the LORD, we have our everlasting Rock. *Isaiah 26:3-4*

The Spirit Himself testifies with our spirit that we are children of God and if children, heirs also, heirs of God and fellow heirs with Christ, if indeed we suffer with Him so that we may also be glorified with Him. For I consider that the suffering of this present time are not worthy to be compared with the glory that is to be revealed to us. *Romans 8:16-19*

"For the mountains may be removed and the hills may shake, But My lovingkindness will not be removed from you, And My covenant of peace will not be shaken," says the LORD who has compassion on you. *Isaiah 54:10*

What's Holding You Back?

It had been a long evening, the conference was over. With only 8 participants it had been a mentally draining workshop. Jerry approached the workshop leader, Dan.

"Thank you Dan for conducting the workshop and all the hard work you put into hosting these. I personally want to thank you for the scholarship in getting me here."
Dan accepted the thank you.

> "But I still don't think that this workshop really applied to me. The other guys had much deeper issues than me. My incident was a one-time deal. I've been able to move on!"
>
> "Do you think that the number of times a person is sexually abused determines the severity of the issues dealt with in adulthood?" Dan asked.
>
> "Well, if your trauma is more severe it means that you will have deeper issues!"

Dan didn't want a long drawn out debate.
> "Jerry, just let me ask you a question or two. If the number of incidents is the key, do you think that your one incident committed against you by your father has helped or hindered your life? Has your life and your family been blessed by his selfish actions?"

Jerry thought for a moment. Tears started streaming down his face.

> "I guess it was abuse...huh. He was the only father I had. There was no one else. If I admitted he betrayed me or disclosed he sexually abused me what would I have left? He raised me. What does that say about me? What does that make me?"

Dan placed his arms around Jerry and embraced him and whispered.

> "Ezekiel 18...you are not responsible for the sins of your father. It's okay to acknowledge his deeds as hurtful and wrong."

Jerry continued to sob. "What do I do? How do I... Where do I..." Dan quieted him.

> "It's okay. You're starting the journey that we talked about on day one, Surrender and Submission. Welcome to the family of Healing Broken men."

There are millions of men like Jerry who are challenged in disclosing and connecting with the reality of the sexual abuse. There are many reasons for non-disclosure and holding the secret. Why are male survivors hesitant and reluctant to disclose? Many claim common reasons like guilt, shame, and embarrassment. These reasons are valid. However, if we probe further we can identify several influential barriers. We have already briefly discussed the difficulties associated with the definition of sexual abuse, but their also exist negative psychological strategies, and detrimental sociocultural stigmas.

Society Plays a Part

Splitting: is also called dissociation, out of body experience. Your mind goes somewhere else until the event is over.

R.W Connell, an Australian sociologist, explains the concept of hegemonic masculinity. This concept conveys that men have been raised to socially dominate other males while overpowering women and having other take subordinate roles. In some cultures this is valid. With defining masculinity today, this may not be the common practice; however it remains the most socially accepted. Hegemonic masculinity conveys the idea that men are expected to be aggressive, strong, winners, emotionally distant, initiators, and independent, power-hungry, competitive and display sexual prowess. From childhood to adulthood, we socialize boys toward possessing these traits. We communicate the expectations in such phrases as: "take it like man and boys don't cry." These expectations herald loudly that men are not victims, especially in the sexual arena.

Male sexual socialization encourages males to define sexual experiences as desirable, provided there is no same-sex involvement. Because of this socialization survivors sometimes refer or define the experience of the sexual abuse as experimentation. One man had such a fear of the negative labels associated with male sexual abuse that he described his incident of repeated anal rape as horseplay. These socio-cultural hegemonic expectations about masculinity generate fear of disclosure. In the survivor's world, disclosure trumpets to society his inability to fit the definition of being a real man. He readily internalizes the blame, grief and false-shame associated with the abuse rather than face possible ostracization. Therefore, the survivor's definition of sexual abuse as contact versus non-contact or less impactful and non-abusive complicates the challenge and lessens the probability of disclosing and seeking therapy. In his reality, embracing the long-term effects and dysfunctional behaviors associated with the abuse are easier to accept than the stigmas received by disclosing. Before we become too discouraged let's bring in a spiritual perspective to address this socialized reality.

Unfortunately, we have allowed such definitions of masculinity to brow beat us into some unrealistic expectations. It is not involvement in sports, sexual prowess, being aggressive, liking sports cars, lifting weights that determine one's masculinity. It's about allowing our character to be the most Christ like as possible. Compassion, nurturing, expressing emotions, quietness, soberness, gentle are wonderful godly characteristics displayed by Jesus, the greatest man to walk this earth. Therefore, before you begin doubting your masculinity based on societal norms, please consider the model of the ultimate man.

Common Obstacles

One of reason healing from the sexual abuse is challenging for men stems from our focus on solely trying to think our way out rather than feel. We have been raised in a society where skills of logic are rewarded but skills of empathy and feeling are disregarded. Logic and clear thinking are considered rationale and normal while feeling and emotion is considered irrational and fickle. The reported traits of male leadership and strength are reason, logic and will ensure success. While emotional expressions are considered feminine, unsafe and out-of-control. Here lies the irony, God made us to be emotional and logical beings however we attempt to separate and dissect the two. A man plagued by the negative effects of the abuse struggles when the emotional issues arise, but he attempts to find logic based solution. This leaves him without the ability and flexibility to resolve his innermost feelings and stifles communication. We often become frustrated because we ask "why and how" concerning our emotions instead of just experiencing them. For centuries men have not been rewarded and approved for feeling but thinking their way out of situations. Fortunately, it doesn't work well in the arena of CSA. Guys are taught to use violence and aggression as their tools of expression. If you want to heal you must venture past logical words only and embrace the feelings of the abuse as you form new behaviors, attitudes and skills in dealing with this problem.

Disclosure

There's a myriad of reason that men are reluctant to disclose. It is challenging to dissect which reason the non-disclosure falls into; social, psychological or familial. As I compose this section of the book, my saddened, frustrated and wounded heart cries for a young man who contacted me this weekend, ready to give up life and hope because his disclosure to his family, friends and church has left him rejected, labeled and condemned. I will plead for forgiveness as I will simply list some of these barriers for delayed disclosure in no particular order.

No cognitive awareness – some men are simply not aware that events that transpired during their childhood. They can identify that something is wrong but often compartmentalize it. We use phrases like "it did not occur to me to tell anybody, I compartmentalized it. I don't have any memories." Awareness is precursor to disclosure and healing.

Intentional unawareness - some men describe intentionally avoiding disclosure of the sexual abuse. Common phrases are "." I blocked it out; I wiped it from my mind." "I didn't want to be aware of it." "I didn't have a need to remember the abuse. I wanted to put it behind."

No Vocabulary – like the child who is abused the adult cannot find the words to describe and expressed what happened. "I didn't know how to explain rape and I still can't." "It was so much more than he's bothering me, but I didn't know how to say it." "I still can't put it into words." "I wanted to but didn't know how to approach it."

Emotionally unready – since we often socialize men to believe that expressing emotions is a sign of weakness it enhances disclosure. "I was afraid of becoming depressed if I told my story." "I just wanted to cry, but wasn't allowed, so I exploded in anger." "the only way to be heard was to be violent." "I couldn't handle the shame." "No one is going to see my cry; they'll think I'm weak." Shame is a double whammy. We experienced shame as men reluctant to share our story. As men not only have issues in expressing our feelings, but also identifying them. We have been socialized from early childhood to not acknowledge sad or painful feelings, especially in the presence of other men.

Become accustomed – as boys sometimes we become so accustomed to the abusive situation that we develop unconventional coping strategies and defensive mechanisms.

We may deny the abuse or distort the reality of the abuse and accept it as normal. Some call it accommodation syndrome.

Emotional attachment to the perpetrator – how could you be attached to a person who betrayed you? Let's go back to that child who needs to receive love and affection from a trusted adult. Who doesn't want to be loved? Even if the only love you received is from your abusive caretaker. As boys we can employ some tactical strategies like dissociating, idealizing, or splitting that we carry into adulthood. Often at the workshops men struggle because they have idealized their familial abuser. By idealizing we can maintain a positive image of the perpetrator and secure a positive attachment.

Displaced blame – as victims we want to desperately maintain that emotional attachment (to be loved) that we displace the blame for the abuse to ourselves. Some victims display Stockholm syndrome, where the development of mutual positive feelings between hostage and captor takes place. This is another form of coping.

Mistrust – is often a common effect of CSA. Since we were betrayed by our trusted protector, no one is above suspicion. In adulthood it can become a paranoid reaction. We often attribute ulterior motives and agendas to those we meet. We never let anyone get close.

Loyalty to family - The more enmeshed the family, the more difficult to disclose the abuse. The level of closeness between the victim and familial perpetrator can be devastating.

Family appearance and integrity – Perpetrators will often use this power technique to persuade, coerce and manipulate the victim into keeping the sexual abuse secret. "If you tell it will break up or destroy your family" "Your parents will blame you and get a divorce" "They will not understand and will hate you."

Fear of being blamed

Rejection and avoidance – men are socially rejected because they are perceived as weak, passive.

Stigma of being gay – this obstacle to disclose sits in the top three. There is negative stigma surrounding CSA committed by another of the same gender. We bypass the real picture of a heinous crime being forced on another human being, and focus on sex. Somehow we equate same gender sexual abuse as a definitive road to sexual orientation.

Intensity of the sexual abuse – The level of trauma can also determine delayed disclosure. We minimize our abuse and feel that it's not impactful therefore disclosure is not necessary. I have witnessed severe traumatic effects from a single incident of abuse.

A study by Sorsoli, Kia-Keating, and Grossman interviewed and recorded the responses of men who struggled with disclosing due to avoidance, inability to articulate, fear of relational issues, and social stigma. I want to share this to help others realize they are not alone. I hear these struggles often at the workshops.

- "I compartmentalized it "/" wasn't aware of it"

- "It never occurred to me to tell"

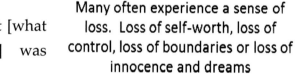

- "I thought [what happened] was normal"

Many often experience a sense of loss. Loss of self-worth, loss of control, loss of boundaries or loss of innocence and dreams

- "I wanted to put it behind me"

- "I wanted to forget it"

- "Don't want to be aware [that it happened]"

- "No need, no purpose, no good reason/ can live with in other ways."

- "I didn't know how to respond (to abuse experience)"
- "I don't know where to start"
- "I don't know how to approach it"
- "I couldn't form the language/ I didn't know the words"
- "I'm not (was not) ready"
- "I knew it (what I did/what happened to me) was wrong"
- "I was being bad (by having it happen/by participating)
- "It was my fault"
- "It's embarrassing/ shameful"
- "I would just get hurt more"
- "It doesn't feel safe"
- "My mother/parents would have sent me away"
- "I didn't want to make things worse" (with mom/parents/siblings)
- "I don't want to be accused of being a rapist, a pervert, gay, crazy"

- "I don't want to hear [someone else's] version of what happened"

- " It f's everything up/ it would be more troubling, cause more problems"

- "I have found talking about emotions to be catastrophic"

- "It's too much, too hard [for people] to hear. It makes [people] feel bad or guilty/they don't comprehend"

- "I don't want to have that kind of closeness"

- "No one talked to me" about things like that/not taught to communicate"

- "I was told to keep it a secret"

- "No one asked me directly"

- "I thought they [parents/teachers/others] already knew"

- "The culture says hush"

- "It's a "taboo" topic"

- "It's not popular to talk about"

> **Sometimes pain is the catalyst that prompts change**

Loved Ones Asked: How can I help him?

Frustration galore! "What do I need to do to help this man? Can't he see that I'm here for him? Why won't he talk?" The voices of countless women and loved ones ring throughout the faith community. People who desire to help a husband, son, brother or boyfriend dealing with CSA. How frustrating to care about a person who was victimized, hurt and betrayed. His hurt becomes your hurt and his pain becomes your pain. Why can't he relate to your sentiments, open up and to let you in?

Reality!

- **You are an important person in his life.** If there is one relationship truth or principle I have learned in dealing with CSA, its "hurting people hurt people". Usually it's not intentional. It's often difficult to meander through the shame, guilt and pain when it's in your face, spinning your world around. Don't take it personal. Our myopic perspective is limited due to pain.

- **Provide unconditional love.** This is one goal as Christians we strive to reflect as part of God's image in us. However, our society exemplifies the concept of conditional or what some call "trick or treat" love. If you treat me right, then I treat you right. However please realize this attitude is detrimental when dealing with a hurting person. As men, the one thing we really need while processing and walking this journey, is unconditional love. A love that says, "I may not be able to relate or understand, but I'm here with you, in whatever way I can effectively serve" This type of love calms the fear of abandonment and the sense of loneliness.

- **Help Him Seek Resources and Counsel.** Okay, guys may act rough and tough on the outside, yet one of our greatest fears as men is being vulnerable and transparent. That deals with the inner man. It's easier to work on the muscles, the physical. It gives us bragging rights. Look what I've accomplished and overcome! Exercising the emotions, fears or despair is more tedious and the results not immediately visible. Therefore it's important for loved ones to realize guys need help finding the resources.

- **Don't nag, nurture and suggest.** Hopefully, we will soon think it was our idea in the first place and do it!

Most guys sign up for the workshop because of the influence or ultimatum of women. Seek help!

- **Realize he may try to ignore, deny and forget his past.** When it comes to burying things, guys beat dogs by a mile. This is often another point of contention and frustration for loved ones. Intuitively or knowingly you have identified dysfunction and hurt in his life. Many of the emails I receive, the marriage has adversely been affected. The spouse can see the effects plain as day but he appears to be clueless. Understand the truth behind our eyes, we don't want to face the past, it's too painful. Realize we are scared and approach with unconditional love, yet lovingly hold us accountable to start the process.

- **Let him move through the stages of denial, anger, acceptance, bargaining, peace, etc**. No person moves through these stages the same way or in the same order. However it's important to realize what stage of the healing process he's currently experiencing.

- **Realize that although hurting, it is never a justifiable excuse to abuse you.** I have coached men in the anger stage who have attempted to physically, verbally use loved ones in their life as a punching bag. Forgive my bluntness, but that's garbage! Yes, we need help and love. However, the love that sometimes needs to be exercised is sound judgment! Love means doing what's right and in the best interest of the person you love. Allowing him to abuse you is not in his best interest or yours.

Take a Break!

Before you continue, stop! Take a walk. Breathe deeply as you walk. Walk for about 15-20 minutes through a park or forest. Enjoy the natural beauty around you. Think about how blessed you are to be finally working through some of the issues. Take a couple of days, weeks whatever you need, to process your journey up to this point.

Pen Action: Take some time to journal what you are experiencing right now.

Chapter Four
Trapped

Unresolved childhood sexual abuse doesn't disappear just because we grow up or decide to ignore it! It's still there and will be manifested in other ways if not addressed.

Male childhood sexual abuse actual has co-existed with female sexual abuse. Throughout history societies have indulge in such tragically perverse behaviors. In various ancient cultures it was practiced without much penalty. In today's world this travesty of abuse continues. However minimal attention to the impact on male children and their adult coping has been acknowledged. As in many things there exists a double standard concerning the abuse of male and female. I must admit the ray hope in approaching this from a faith perspective is to realize that in God's perspective there is not male or female, Jew or Greek...(Galatians 3:28) but hurting souls that need help. Many attitudes toward masculinity and maleness have hampered ascertaining information and help for male survivors leaving countless numbers of men and their loved ones trapped in endless peril. Myths and negative social stereotypes have created reluctance for scared boys to report the sexual abuse during childhood and terrified men to seek help in adulthood. Even parents are conflicted and reluctant to seek assistance for their boys. This underreporting demonstrates the psychological conflict caused by society's askew definition of masculinity that many in the religious arenas also believe. Society imbues the perception that a man's role as initiator and aggressor of any sexual activity or interest is the norm. Therefore male sexual abuse survivors we are trapped with great challenges. Their abuse is unacceptable because they are the recipient, men are not dominated, and they are the dominators. Men are not victims. If the sexual abuse was perpetrated by the same gender this disgrace and disrespect to his manhood tarnishes him because he has been involved in a homosexual act. If he was sexually abused by a female and considered it not pleasureable his masculinity is also called into question.

Yes, it seems ridiculous to require a young child with no understanding of life, sex and anything else to protect and defend his masculinity or manhood from the grown adult who sexually abuses him. However in essence that's exactly what we have done. If they are really men they should be strong enough to protect themselves. Men are protectors. To admit being abused is seen as a sign of weakness, unmasculine and it becomes a "blame the victim" situation. Piled on top of this notion is also the reality that men have been socialized early in life to conceal any emotional and physical vulnerabilities and weakness.

Why mention this? I mention it because it is often these underlying socialized perceptions of masculinity that assists in producing men trapped with long-term sexual abuse effects like anxiety, confusion, post traumatic syndrome, shame, guilt, inability to be intimate, fear of expressing feelings, sexual dysfunction, compulsive disorders, insomnia, esteem issues, hypervigilence, substance abuse, inability to trust, gender issues, identity crisis, anger management, overachievers, social alienation, suicidal thoughts, negative body image, addictions, depression, pornography and verbal, emotional abuse, only to name a few. If you think this is a travesty, now introduce a religious moral community that accentuates and focuses on sex being bad. You have created a boy who grows into a man who will face one of the greatest internal battles ever fought in his life. That is the reality.

What did I lose?

I can remember growing watching the family shows on TV, the Cosby Show being one of my favorite. It was a perfect world and fit nice and neatly into the myth of "childhood is the best years of your life". Unless you are part of a different reality that sends conflicting messages of love, betrayal, trust, pain and abuse.

Adult males often internalize the "badness" of the experience and interpret their role in the abuse from a child's perspective, believing somehow they were bad.

It's a world where you have no power and must endure imposed rules and regulations without any clear understanding or explanation. You are expected to obey, taught not to question elders or authority, to be compliant and to simply carry out the orders. This defined a perfect child. If only I could have slightly changed that view instilled in me years ago, maybe things would have been slightly different. The problem is that as survivors we cannot go back and change the events that shaped us, nor can we fully recount and recover the losses.

Loss Childhood

Many have buried childhood memories of the abuse. This often can be a defense mechanism for dealing with extremely difficult situations. I have found that portions of my memories are scattered. If you asked for my memories from age six to thirteen, I struggled to produce any. Before working through these issues, I could only produce some memories up to age six and others after age fourteen. As I began to unravel the mysteries of my lost years, I found that gigantic gaps occurred during the time the abuse took place.

Some adult survivors have created strategies for protection from these painful memories. They may exhibit selective amnesia, denial, or even rewrite childhood history into perfect memoirs. When asked about childhood and family, the picture perfect family is painted. Oh, they may throw in a couple of flaws to fit in with the rest of the crowd, but in their made-up world, childhood was good. They have chosen to re-remember the creative version of their childhood, in order to function.

Lost childhood—often during the workshop male survivors will report a gap of time during their childhood. During the years of the sexual abuse the child utilizes the resilient power of memory to forget, deny and block and survive the abusive situation. We tend to remember the positive good things of childhood.

Survivors from the workshop shared their losses

- **Loss of Trust** – my innate nature to trust is gone, I'm suspicious of everyone

- **Loss of nurturing environment** –this doesn't feel nurturing. No one will ever touch me again.

- **Loss of self-concept, esteem** -- I'm bad, it's my fault that he chose me.

- **Loss of sexual maturation** –I was awakened to the pain of sexual violation. I don't understand how sex, love and violence are different. The first time will never be special for me.

- **Loss of security**—I can't count on protection. No matter where I go, I'm always looking over my shoulder.

- **Loss of safety**

- **Loss of control** –I'm so afraid that I'll lose it and my anger will consume me. Then I'll hurt someone

- **Loss of a sense of belonging** –I'm marked for life. I will always been seen as different and I cannot regain

- **Loss of being normal** –even if it doesn't really exist, I'll never have a chance a knowing what normal could have been.

- **Loss of just learning to play** – I never experienced just the fun stuff that kids do. My life now is so serious

- **Loss the ability to learn to build healthy friendships** - I isolated myself for protection. Never learned to build social bonds and relationships.

- **Loss of my innocence** - I didn't have a say in when I wanted to give my innocence away.

- **Loss of tranquility** –life has been so chaotic since that moment in time. Never a time to mentality rest

- **Loss of my masculinity**—I just can't feel normal around other guys. I can't even go camping with my kid and sleep in the same tent. All my friends and acquaintances are female because I don't trust other men.

Does the sense of loss disappear as we age? We can surmise from the above responses that the losses do not disappear but affects survivors well into their adult years. I remember studying and becoming a martial arts fanatic. My college roommates would walk into my room and fall to their knees to pay homage to my Bruce Lee shrine. Yes, I enjoyed martial arts. However, the overkill represented my attempt to deal with hurt and loss; I was attempting to fight back. As a survivor you will feel robbed and cheated of life and happiness as you put the pieces of your abuse puzzle together. What is to keep you going? Realizing that you cannot find what is lost or missing until you discover it is missing or lost.

Lies Destroys

Much of the sexual abuse that boys encounter is not a single incident, but rather a prolonged period of multiple incidents.

However, whether it was a single incident or prolonged chronic abuse, his belief structure is shattered. He is stamped with the idea that people are not trustworthy. They abuse, exploit, and hurt. They lie and deceive. Also, the boy's self-concept of being a man often has been traumatically altered. His mindset and behavior in every relationship he encounters going forward is skewed. Even in adulthood, his relationships are tainted with mistrust. His inner circle may consist of an army of one, himself. His life may feel unfulfilled and incomplete with the intimacy he desires. He has experienced distorted values. He learned that violence in relationships is normal, sex equates to love, and being distant provides safety and protection. He has discovered that rape is normal. The effect of these lies created pain that continued to into adulthood. Never trust men or women. For me, fearing and distrusting any type of intimacy placed me in isolation and because of my feelings of rejection, I was unable to connect with people.

Other ramifications of abuse may incline the abused toward frequent, short-lived, or volatile relationships. This stage is a little better than isolation, but due to our suspicious nature, and the possibility of rejection, we invest no quality time in our relationships. We mistrust words and the actions of others. Candid, open communication does not exist. When confronted with problems in relationships, we use silence, or hostility, and withdraw into ourselves. We blame others for our failed relationships. We often think, "I knew he couldn't be trusted!" Or, "She would hurt me." Similar to domestic abuse survivors, we sometimes enter a relationship that recreates the abusive victim mentality for us. It feels comfortable. We are familiar with the scripted behavior pattern. We trap ourselves in a cycle. The ramifications and results of the sexual abuse can be overwhelming, but with God's help, the desire to change, and the fortitude to work, we can find new life.

Xavier Shares

"People called me a faggot. I liked to read books, cook, and plant things, geeky or nerdy things by today's terms. They labeled me as a sensitive boy, which boys were not allowed to be during that time. My relatives were always attempting to make me into a real man. I was supposed to be tough and rough. I barely was a teenager. The parents constantly dragged me to sports events to try and get me interested in them. They just wanted me to fit in so I didn't look like a weird child. I hated it! Couldn't they accept me for me? Everyone was attempting an extreme makeover on me. They didn't see me as macho boy or man material, and were trying very hard to shape a piece of dry clay. If only they could have seen what was happening to me inside, I was dying, and whoever I really wanted to be was ignored. I was really confused. My abuser was different. He was really attentive and friendly, and told me everything was okay. He said that no one would find out about what we were doing. That was a comfort, because I couldn't handle being different any more. He tapped into what I needed. He talked with me about the books I read. He seemed to accept me for me. He was the only one attending to that part crying out to be loved. In a distorted way I trusted him; I thought that I loved him as father figure. I understand now that it was all a lie. That hurts tremendously, because what I thought was love really was not. God please help me.

Pen Action:

1. How has your self-concept of being a man been affected by the abuse?

2. How does it feel to struggle alone while working through your issues of abuse?

3. List ways in which the abuse affects your relationships

Prayer:

Lord, you are a God of truth. Help me to deal with the truth of abuse in my life. Help me to trust You and fill my life with others I can trust to help me. If there is pride in my heart to attempt this alone, purge it from me. Lord, help me to realize that You created us to be in relationship with You and others.

> **Principle: Bocked Healing**
> Sometimes pride becomes and idol and hinders our healing. Our struggle involves matters of the heart. Wehn we half heartedly believe in god's word and promis to help us, we limit the blessing He has for our life.

Dreaming A New World

Sexually abused boys sometimes utilize fantasy as a protective and defensive mechanism. Some boys run away from home and become street transients. Some are forced or coerced into child prostitution as a means of survival. For those who can not run away, sometimes the world of fantasy helps to cope with the horrific abuse. Perhaps as a survivor you may find this story similar to your own

Mike Shares

I wanted to have a perfect family, the type of family my friend Jason had. Jason and his dad played baseball and catch. Sometimes they rough housed in the yard. His mom read stories, baked my favorite cookies, and tucked me into bed with a sweet kiss when I slept over. That was the type of life I experienced at Jason's house. What a cool family! I invented every possible excuse to be at Jason's home. I often dreamed and fantasized that Jason's family was my own. They didn't attend church like my family, but somehow they were better. They were the way a family should be. Each time after my abuse, I daydreamed and pretended Jason's family was my family. It was easier for me to deal with the abuse by pretending. I pretended that Jason's dad was my real father. He wouldn't do such things to hurt me.

Prayer:

(Unknown Author)

God, make me brave for life: oh, braver than this.
Let me straighten after pain, as a tree straightens after the rain, Shining and lovely again.
God, make me brave for life; much braver than this.
As the blown grass lifts, let me rise
From sorrow with quiet eyes,
Knowing Thy way is wise.
God, make me brave, life brings
Such blinding things.
Help me to keep my sight;
Help me to see aright
That out of dark comes light.

Making Excuses is Easier

As a child, your perpetrator may have threatened, coerced or manipulated you into never talking about your abuse. In some instances parents may have expressed disdain and silenced you to not discuss this family problem. Or you may have instinctly learned that revealing the secret brings more chaos, hurt and pain. I remember being told by one of my abusers instilling the fear that my parents would be angry and punish me for being involved in such behavior. John shared at the workshop how his mother taught him to masturbate and the sexual acts she perpetrated against him.

Many viewed John as a man's man. He had climbed the corporate success later and his indedpendent wealth made him the envy of others. He was the poster child for turning rags into riches. His father had sexually abused him and his sister. Sometimes the abuse resulted physical pain and blood. He didn't shed a tear. John toughed it out like a real man. His father would often voice. John had learned to numb the feelings of his abuse. John was unshakable in his adult years. He experienced a string of unfortunate events. His wife left him after ten years of marriage and they battled for custody for the love of his life, the kids. His mother died a year later. His sister developed sistemic cancer of the lymph nodes and died within three months. John lost part of his wealth in trusting his accountant who embezzled funds. John had a strong spiritual life as a youth director and project manager for regional praise conferences. No sweat and not a single tear with all the tragedy. One night during a group dinner while slicing the brocolli for the stir-fry, he cut his finger. The cut bled for about thirty seconds, then stopped. All of a sudden he began to cry. The sight of the blood took him back to his father's abuse. He cried uncontrolably through the night and the next day. He cried thirty-five years of tears. The floodgates had been open and their was no more denying or minimizing.

John represents millions of male survivors who deny their abuse because admitting or acknowledging the event involves touching a myriad of painful feelings. The best way to avoid pain and discomfort is to block it. John felt ambivalent. There were negative and positive feelings about the father who abused him. John always covered for his father's behavior trying to rationalize or minimize the abuse by making excuses. "Dad couldn't help it. He was abused as a child, too." Or, "Mom was an alcoholic. She didn't really realize what she was doing with the drugs. She had a horrible childhood, a lousy marriage, and manic depression." Such excuses helped to block the pain and reality of bad abusive behavior. Often as male survivors we dampen the severity of the abuse by telling ourselves, "It could have been worse compared to…" Yet, if someone shared with us that a child was being abused in the same manner today, we would be irate and react with vehement anger. We have denied, blocked, and minimized our traumatic feelings.

Minimize and Deny

> Often our denial gets in the way of acknowledging what is going on inside. You may minimize your abuse if it was not blatant, painfully brutal or experienced one incident

Early childhood or late

When talking with others, I often find that whether the sexual abuse occurred early in childhood or later both are quite traumatic and negatively impact the survivor's life. Some reports advocate the more traumatic the incident, the greater the impact. However that also is quite subjective as each survivor copes differently. Much of the reported abuse occurs before puberty. Some studies lean towards the idea that the greater the age difference between the child and the perpetrator, the greater negative impact. This too is subjective. I have encountered men sexually abused by perpetrators only a couple of years their senior that have left some very traumatic effects. The gist of the story is "Sexual abuse of a child is traumatic at any age, perpetrated by whoever." No wonder our brains want to subconsciously numb and lose these traumatic years.

Pen Action:

- Can you remember at what age your abuse began?

- If you can how old were you?

- Do you feel the sexual abuse was violent, threatening, or coercive?

- Was it subtle, or manipulative?

- How long did the abuse last?

- How frequent did the abuse occur?

- What was your relationship with the abuser? Was she/he a relative, or someone else?

- Did anyone else know of the abuse?

- How did others respond to knowledge of you being abused?

- Do you have pictures, or can you picture yourself before the abuse?

- How did you look?

- Do you remember a change or shift in appearance during the time of the abuse?

- What is the range of emotions you experience when recalling lost memories?

Rationalizations we may attempt to claim

- I didn't stop it…therefore I must have……
- I had a lot of problems so…
- My parents had it rough…
- People during my generation…
- I was a difficult child…
- I was asking for it with my behavior…
- She didn't know what she was doing…
- I was too needy as a kid…
- He needed someone to love since mom wouldn't
- I must have seduced…
- He just couldn't help it..
- It was because of his alcoholism…

> **Rationalization,** which is another form of denial means we can think our way out of feeling the real pain associated with the abuse.

Prayer:

God, as I remember the abuse that was committed against me, please supply me strength to face it honestly. Please help me work through these issues truthfully, and with courage. Help me to unlock the past, so I can heal my present, and look forward to a wonderful future. Grant me the peace that can only come through having an intimate relationship with you.

> **Truths and Promises**
>
> "These things I have spoken to you, so that in Me you may have peace. In the workld you have tribulation but take courage; I have overcome the world" *John 16:33*
>
> In peace I will both lie down and sleep, For You alone, O LORD, make me to dwell in safety *Psalm 4:8*
>
> How lovely on the mountains are the feet of him who brings good new, Who announces peace and brings good news of happiness, who announces salvation, and says to Zion, "Your God reigns!" *Isaiah 52:7*

Just My thoughts: Why Recall Memories Now?

You may wonder why it has taken so long to get around to recalling memories. Once again, you are not alone. Many men start dealing with these problems in their late thirties, forties or even their fifties. I was in my thirties when I started working through them. I needed to create some distance between the place and location where my abuse took place. It's difficult to explain, but subconsciously I knew I had to leave those familiar surroundings in order to have a fighting chance to begin healing.

Another reason you may you may be recalling memories now is that you feel somewhat safe. Healing takes place in a safe environment. You may now have Christian friends or family who offer you acceptance, people who are ready for your pain, and can help with healing.

The need to trust others is essential. This can be very difficult for guys, due to certain stereotypes and societal norms placed on us. We labor to overcome fear of rejection. We house suspicion. We need to overcome these barriers. The most powerful work overcoming obstacles facing survivors is in safe environments. This is one reason I try to encourage others to attend the workshop. They can rest in a safe environment, and meet others with similar issues.

Another reason for working through the issues later is emotional readiness. If there is one factor as male survivors we must realize, it is that healing takes place in emotional unload. The importance of expression of feelings is monumental. We live in a society that believes that real men don't cry. Don't you believe it!

Of the Old Testament bible characters, Joseph is one of the most outstanding. He's authentic, the real deal, a real man. When he forgave the sins of his brothers, who mistreated him, he cried more than any other Bible character. As male survivors, we need to cry, tremble, and sob, because it is the outward manifestation of the grief and pain we have experienced.

Maybe we did not cry as children. We didn't have a safe environment a protector to rely upon, so we could not be vulnerable. Some of our abusers became more brutal or became enraged if we cried. We had to "take it like a man." Now that we are older, we can find a place of security.

Now may be the time because something has triggered your memories. Some of my memories came back while watching a movie. A scene involved a person being abused. I also have known men whose memories were triggered by the birth of their son; a baby these men became very adamant about protecting. In my experience as a certified licensed massage therapist, men have cried uncontrollably on the massage table, because they felt the nurtured by someone who didn't want to hurt them in any way.

When you are ready, allow the emotional unload to take place. Have your network of support in place. Don't feel embarrassed and attempt to cover up the pain. Get rid of the baggage!

Finding Safe People to Connect With

Pen Action:

- Name people you are connected with

- Name several friends you might feel comfortable talking to about your abuse.

- Name one or more friends who are sympathetic.

- Name one or more friends who are caring.

- Name one or more friends who have great listening skills.

- Name one or more friends who are logical.

- Name one more friends who are good huggers.

- Name one or more friends who are great problem solvers.

- Name one or more friends who are nonjudgmental (condemning).

- Name one or more friends who are good at knowing how to apply appropriate scriptures to different circumstances.

- Name one or more friends who can rejoice when you rejoice, and mourn when you mourn.

- Name one or more friends who can be trusted with your confidential information.

- Name one or more friends who are optimistic.

Flashbacks

Flashbacks can occur at any time. They can be triggered by a sound, image, smell or even touch. They are troublesome intrusive memories of the painful event. They often leave us frightened, dishoveled and confused. Please understand they are a normal part of the healing process. This might seem counter-intuitive but it's good when these memories begin to surface. I believe it represents your psyche being open to the healing process. Dreams like flashbacks are valuable tools of healing depending on how we relate to them; with fear and intrepidation or embracing to understand. Why are men so afraid of them? They are unpredictable and uncontrollable. They give no warning. Therefore the key is to have the correct attitude and skills to address them.

Flashbacks are recalled memories from the past. They often are manifested or triggered in the form of smells, pictures, images, dreams, sounds. Sometimes there is no visual or auditory recall but feelings. During the time of the childhood sexual abuse your body and mind used whatever means at its disposal to protect you emotionally from the abuse: memory suppression, numbness to feelings...etc. It was difficult experiencing such a horrific situation. Unable to express and disclose the feelings during the actual abuse our child voice remained locked inside.

As we experience the flashbacks and feelings we might venture to think we are crazy. We feel out of control especially if panic attacks are involved. The unique quality about emotions and feelings is that they are not time limited. As we start to experience the past that has been locked away for years it emerges as if it were happening today. The switch occurs. The childhood self re-emerges with the unresolved issues. To us the feelings and sensations seem to come from out of the blue. Before you convince yourself that you are crazy, let me share the fact that flashbacks are normal. Flashbacks are often part of Post-Traumatic Stress Disorder. It often helps to remind yourself that you are having a flashback. Today, 30 years later, I sometimes experience flashbacks of the unwanted sexual contact. When this occurs it's important to for me to breathe, keep myself grounded, re-establish boundary parameters between past and present, not punish myself and allow myself to experience the pain and hurt, to find safe help and share. The memories, flashbacks, and feelings represent the body's coping mechanism. When triggered, like a time machine they transport us back to when the abuse first took place.

Why Do They Feel So Real?

I will attempt to explain this as simple as possible. There are two types of memory, explicit and implicit. Explicit memory you recall facts, info and you are conscious or aware that you are recalling or remembering it. Internally you control bringing up the memories. Implicit memory is recorded sensations, emotional experiences, feelings associated with an event that are automatically recalled. One is not aware or purposely thinks about them. The

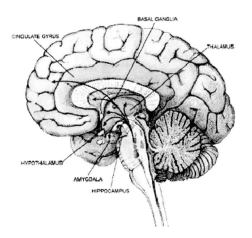

implicit memories are laid down by our limbic system. The limbic system are brain structures located at the top of the brainstem and underneath the cortex. These structures are involved in our emotions and motivations like fear, anger and emotions related to sexual behavior. This area is also responsible for feelings of survival and pleasure. There are two important structures, the amygdala and hippocampus. The amygdala determines what memories are stored in the brain. The hippocampus packages the memories and sends them to the appropiate hemisphere for long-term storage and retrival. Trauma is recorded in the limbic system. The hippocampus takes the feelings, thoughts, and emotions and consolidates them in a narrative which becomse your life story. If the thoughts, feelings, emotions are never consolidated and converted by the hippocampus into the biographic package, then you experience the memory as if it is happening to you right now. That's when you experience the flashback. According to your brain you are right back at that time an moment experiencing the fear, fright, hurt, pain, you are in the moment. Since this structure sits atop the vagus nerve and brain stem it controls some primary functions. Your body releases the cortisol (fight and flight hormone) so you react, freeze, run, feel scared, heart races, mood regulated, shortness of breathe as if the bear is right there chasing you, eventhough it was 10 years ago. Implicit memories are not tied to context, time and place.

Working with Flashbacks

Try not to force and suppress the thoughts and images. Allow yourself to experience these feelings and images as they surface. Various studies report that continually ignoring, suppressing or trying to deny the abuse actually make it worse now and in the long term. Personally I have found it useful to say to myself, "It's okay to experience these thoughts and feelings. Let it flow for now and when it feels too much stop and revisit it later." This allows me some control, but also helps me to realize that this is a continual process. Allow someone who is safe to experience the thoughts and feelings with you. This was one of the reasons for establishing the workshops for survivors. There is a liberating power in being able to share the feelings and thoughts with some safe. Journal those things that seem to trigger the feelings, thoughts and memories. This will provide better insight into self and how to handle your situation.

Flashbacks Make Me Sexless

It is not unusual for male survivors to experience times when sexual interest or contact with their spouse is undesired. This can be traumatic for both in the relationship. Some men are dealing with severe trauma any type of sexual intercourse or contact elicits such strong flashbacks, feelings of shame, disgust and hurt that it makes physical intimacy a serious challenge. The best advice I can share with you on this scenario is to lovingly let your partner know it's not a personal issue with her. She is not the cause. . It can be particularly difficult for incest victims and males who have been abused by males.

Continual Tears

As you experience the flashbacks it often produces bouts of tears. For guys we have been socialized to believe that guys don't cry. Please don't believe it. At the workshops guys often share they are frustrated with themselves which cause even more emotions to surface. One survivor shared his road to working through the issues. He would cry after sex each time and could not understand why. Sometimes we will cry for what seems like no apparent reason. During these times it's key to have someone to share with you what you are feeling or to say what you are feeling to God. Put it out there! The reason I encourage you to share stems from the fact that constantly being in this mental state is not healthy and could lead to deep depression. Tears are great form of emotional cleansing and purging. However, extreme emotional purging can be detrimental. It is important to have encouragers in your life during the stages of grief and tears.

When Love Is on the Line!

Intimacy normally presents some great challenges, but coupled with the long-term effects of childhood sexual abuse it can be devastating. Do you keep the abuse from your spouse or soon to be? How many do you share? Let me share with you from personal experience.

Everyone wants to belong, be accepted and loved. Rejection is not usually a desirable outcome. In those first dating days or honeymoon phase, we don't want to upset or rock the boat. We always attempt to put our best side forward, not acknowledge the pain, hurt and dysfunction. Although it might seem easier to continue to keep the secret of your abuse, I would not recommend it. If there is one sentiment that I often hear from wives who lovingly insist their husbands attend the workshops, it is "I didn't sign-up for this!" This thought resonates through many marriages where male childhood sexual abuse has occurred and the couple is working through many of the issues.

If I'm involved in a relationship when should I share?

My suggestion is based on my own experience, and the easiest and hardest four letter word in relationships can be W-A-I-T! As the relationship becomes closer sometimes it becomes more difficult to disclose and share because we fear rejection, and loss. Keeping silent is easier. At the same time I do not suggest disclosing early in the dating stage but waiting until the relationship moves toward life-time committed to each other. Having said that I must also add, you need to determine if you are ready for being involved in a committed relationship. It can be very challenging, strenuous and difficult to maintain a relationship and working through PTSD, childhood abuse issues. Don't overextend yourself. As time progresses and the relationship grows, you may desire to share the abuse because you don't want to keep secrets. The wonderful news is that most people want to help, comfort, and support and love you. When a spouse shares the comment that "I didn't sign-up for this" they often are expressing the feeling that the issue is too big for them to handle alone and are requesting the male survivor to seek more help.

Exodus

There also exists another reality and one I have experienced. The ring was never placed on the finger or the spouse leaves. It hurts. I felt rejected, condemned and frustrated. I felt as if I was being punished, and judged as the criminal for a crime committed against me. Yes there will be some partners that will leave. There are others unwilling to form or continue in relationship with a person who has been sexually abused. As much as it hurt, I realized that everyone cannot handle or help carry this burden. I would rather have a person who is committed to the relationship knowing the unpleasant details about me. To me sharing life means sharing the uncomfortable as well as the comfortable. Yet, at the same time, I would not expect my spouse to be my therapist/counselor.

Sorry if that excerpts seemed out of place. It was on my mind as I thought about flashbacks and some of the areas in which they have affected my life relationships and I just wanted to share them with you in case you have traveled down this road also. At the workshop we also discuss how sexual abuse can fuel or influence addictions. You are not alone.

> **Truths and Promises**
>
> A man of too many friends comes to ruin, but there is a friend who sticks closer than a brother. *Proverbs 18:24*
>
> As iron sharpens iron, so one man sharpens anotherl *Proverbs 27:17*
>
> A Friend loves at all times and a brother is born of adversity. *Proverbs 17:17*
>
> Rejoice with those who rejoice, and weep;with those who weep. *Romans 12:15*

Principle: Set Expectations

The exercise you just completed helps you identify friends and develop a support group. As you work through the abuse and share with others, you must set the expectations and boundaries by being clear on what you need from your support group. If you need a listener, then request it. If you need a shoulder to cry on, then request it. If you need a problem solver, then request it. Your friends will probably want to help you.

Let me provide an example how to ask someone to be part of your support group. You can say, "Thanks for sharing some of your time with me. I really need a friend who can listen to me right now. It might get a little emotional at times for me, I'm not sure. If you feel you can help me with this I would really appreciate it." If you have people who just don't get it, then feel free to share this little poem.

> **Listen**
>
> Please listen! All that I ask is that you listen – not talk or do something for me – just hear me. When I ask you to listen, please do nto start giving me advice; this is not what I'm requesting. When I ask you to listen, please do nto scold me, or say I shouldn't feel the way I do. Let me express the feelings I have. When I ask you to listen, resist the urge to solve my problem. I am not hopeless or helpless – maybe jsut discouraged, or hurt. So, please listen and just hear me. I promise youthat ifyou want to talk, wait a minute for your turn. Then, I'll listen to you.

Reasons We Don't Disclose

- A cultural bias maintains that males cannot be victims. Males are expected to be confident, knowledgeable, and aggressive. To be a victim means one is an inadequate male

- If the boy's body has responded sexually, he feels he is somehow responsible for the sexual abuse

- Male victims of sexual abuse struggle with issues of homosexuality as most offenders are male. Their homophobia plus their confusion and fear encourage silence. Not to mention the social stigma attached to homosexuality

- Boys fear negative judgment by family and friends

Just a Few Facts

- Researchers surveyed 1,213 grade 6 - 8 students at To-ronto area schools on whether they had been a victim of unwanted sex behaviors in the previous 6 weeks: 22% of males reported having been victimized (Blackwell, 20023)
- Canadian estimates have shown that there are close to five million male victims of sexual abuse, most of which are unwanted sexual touching (Matthews, 1996, p. 154)
- In one study of 30 male victims of sexual abuse, the aver-age age at the first time of abuse was 8 years, 4 months (Dorais, 2002, p. 1848).

- In a Los Angeles Times poll conducted in 1990 with 2,626 men and women over 18 years of age, Finkelhor and Associates (19905) discovered that 16% of the men recalled a history of sexual abuse. The median age for these male victims was 9.9 years of age (as cited in Wiehe, 1998, p. 21)

Scared Boys Terrified Men|

Take a Break!

Before you continue, stop! Take a walk. Breathe deeply as you walk. Walk for about 15-20 minutes through a park or forest. Enjoy the natural beauty around you. Think about how blessed you are to be finally working through some of the issues. Take a couple of days, weeks whatever you need, to process your journey up to this point.

Scared Boys Terrified Men|

Pen Action: Take a little time and space here to write about what you are experiencing right now!

Cry of the Hurting

Years of agony and years of pain, the incredible horrific guilt
of the sexual abuse and shame reign.

I ponder and wonder what life could have been for me,
endless tiring dreams and fantasies of what will never be.

Comparing myself to others who will never understand, why
it hurts and kills me to try and shape myself into the world's
picture of a stereotypical man.

I ask for help to pick up the pieces wherever they may fall,
and continue to yell into the abyss of darkness hoping
someone will answer my call.

- Thomas Edward

Chapter Five
Sex and Identity

So God created man in his own image, in the image of God he created him; male and female he created them. And God blessed them. And God said to them, "Be fruitful and multiply and fill the earth and subdue it, and have dominion over the fish of the sea and over the birds of the heavens and over every living thing that moves on the earth." Genesis 1:27–28 (ESV)

Sex Is a Bad Word

One reason dealing with male childhood sexual abuse in the Christian community presents a great challenge is that the subject involves sex.

Sex! Okay, we said it!

Unfortunately mentioning the word still does not remove the shock value or taboo surrounding the subject. Sex unfortunately is often demonized in various Christian circles and often produces a knee-jerk reaction of uneasiness when discussed. Enormous emphasis has been placed on the physical act causing many to lose sight of the abuse. The problem has never been sex. God created it and approved it. It was not made to be a bad, dirty, or shameful act.

Unfortunately, it is often portrayed that way in some religious circles. Some believers dare not touch the Song of Solomon because it talks about...shhh...don't say it too loud, "Sex!" Yet it celebrates God-given desires in the unions of men and women everywhere, and supplies them another opportunity for closeness and intimacy resembling the divine nature of the godhead. In our faith perspective, when sex is taken out of its proper godly context of marriage then it becomes twisted into illicit behaviors like: fornication, adultery, bestiality, rape, incest, or sexual abuse.

The victim of the sexual abuse is not the culprit. The abuser/perpetrator who defiled God's intent for sex is the culprit, by using it in a selfish unrighteous manner. Since so much emphasis has been placed on the sexual act, the victim often takes on the shame, guilt, and agony associated with the crime committed against him. Sex is very powerful. It involves body, mind and emotions. We can understand why God reserved it for marriage. However, guys who experience sexual abuse often associate sex with anger and fear, guilt and shame, physical pain, confusion and secrecy.

Internal Messages

Personality development studies often cite that during our stages of development from child to adolescence to adult our concept and view of self is greatly influenced by the messages we receive from others. This means that our concept of self and esteem are constructed from our relationships with others. As stated before I believe that value and worth come from external sources and then are internalized. In sexual abuse, the act of sex is demonized and considered bad. The child has no real concept or context for the sex but realizes it is bad. Now that he has been forced, manipulated, coerced, threatened but involved in the act, he relates to the object, sex is bad, therefore he is bad. Interestingly enough object theory supports the idea that from a psychological perspective the concerns over goodness and badness never really disappear. It presents a constant battle with shame and guilt even when addressed in therapy and counseling. This is where I believe faith for the believer plays an important part in healing. The shame and guilt which really is not his to own can be laid at the feet of another object or person, Jesus. (Romans 8:1- There is no condemnation...) Yes, some may coin this as a crutch, but when you are broken a crutch is what one needs to provide support. That's how faith helps us. Perhaps if we allowed more individuals to see believers broken also, but utilizing Jesus as part of the solution we would be greater witnesses (just my personal three cents). The ability to restore self-esteem could be established by strengthened true value into the man's idealized self (Psalm 8:4-5 what is man that...).

Perspective

Rape is an intrusive crime carried out through sexual means. I remember as a child walking home from school and being bit by a dog. It instilled my psyche with terror, fear and hatred of dogs. When I adopted a little husky puppy from the senior center nursing home at the age of nine, raising the animal curb some of my apprehension. However, today as an adult I enjoy playing with puppies and will rub the head of a dog occasionally, but dogs can still be objects of terror for me. The sight of a grown dog, especially Dobermans' makes me feel uncomfortable. It probably should not, but it does. That's my experience. My connection is a childish one that has been unconsciously carried into my adult life. If you understand that illustration then instead of a child and a dog, introduce a child and sexual abuse in whatever form, as we discussed earlier. The caring trusted adult violates the child by sexually victimizing him. Adults are supposed to be protectors, nurturers and safe, but they become the perpetrators. Like me with dogs, the child learns to mistrust, second guess and fear adults who show caring, protective overtones, which subconsciously feel like his sexual victimization experience. Usually the associations are not consciously made, but the pathways or connections exist. Whether these childhood perceptions are true, accurate or not, they are incorporated into our adult worldview and determine how we respond.

David Shares

"My life feels ruined and hopeless at times. No one can touch me or flatter me, because I misconstrue it as sexual ulterior motives. I assume that the only reason a person likes me is because he/she want sexual favors from me. Of course, it's hard to live in a world and not be touched.

It's so confusing to really understand what I feel. I want to be made whole. A simple hug from a caring friend would be a blessing. If I could just break through this barrier, I know the risk would be worth it. Sometimes I become so enraged. I didn't ask for this garbage. It was handed to me by a man who had a different idea of love. The strangeness is that I will not allow any men to touch me or be close--and this is what I really long for. I wish it could have been the arms of my dad rescuing me from the grips of uncle's distorted version of love, but he did nothing. It was his brother. Dad had no time for me. I'd give my life for a hug by a male figure that loves me and just wants to be my friend. I pray for that day."

David has received incorrect information concerning loving touch, caring relationships and sex. David now assumes that any expression of caring, helping or protection will lead to sex. All touch in his world is interpreted as sexual. If his abuse involved violence then touch to him might represent violence. Now that this misinformation has been incorporated into his life, he approaches and responds to his world by fearing and avoiding forms of caring expression. If this does not seem devastating to a family let me share a call I received.

Corey called at 1:00 a.m. His voiced sounded frantic and desperate.

"My son has been looking forward to this camping trip for years. It's like a rite of passage." Corey breathed hard.

I took out my notepad to scribble a few notes to keep myself awake. Corey did not have time to waste and at o'clock in the morning with a presentation to give at a conference in a few hours, I could somewhat relate.

"Corey you said that this camping trip with your son has been in the works for 3 years? It's something that the dad's at your congregation do with their sons when they reach eleven? Your son has been excited about this excursion for over a year. Therefore it really means a lot to him and you don't want to let him down?"

"Yes. That correct. However, the camp is tomorrow and I just cannot go through with this! I can barely tuck my son into bed at night lately. My boy likes to snuggle against me. It makes him feel safe, but I feel uncomfortable. He's dealing with some bullying. I'm trying to be supportive.

"You will never find time for anything. If you want time, you must make it."
– Charles Bixton

"Okay that's understandable."

"Yeah, but if freaks me out and I start having panic attacks. It's bringing up some triggers and flashbacks of being sexually abused as a child for me." Corey sobbed. "I don't want to mess this up for my son, if I don't go on this trip it could really ruin our strained relationship, but I can't do this I need to call it off."

"Corey what happens when your son snuggles against you when you tuck him in? What do you experience? What do you feel? How long does it last?"

"I start feeling like the room is closing in on me, it becomes hard to breath, claustrophobic and I need air. Sometimes I open the window or turn the fan on to make it better."

I did not have time to inquire about the extent of his sexual abuse, but definitely could relate to panic smothering feeling. "Corey what did your therapist say."

"Look man! He doesn't get it! He can't relate to being sexually abused and feeling that presence of a 200lb body on top of me, not being able to breathe while being sexually abused. You can because you have experienced it! Will you help me or not?"

From his tone, I determined this was majorly important to Corey and his relationship with his son was hanging in the balance. "Corey let me give you my disclaimer. I'm not a licensed therapist yet and this is not treatment. I'm a Christian life coach and you are asking me for some advice based on my personal experience and working with other men at workshops…etc… Correct?"

"Yes, advice! Whatever I don't care! I'm not planning on suing you. Please for the love of God help me. I take whatever advice you suggest into consideration."

My heart could not take anymore. This man needed my help. If my motto "that it's not about the number of letters behind a person's name that counts, but if they genuinely care, and will help" was true this was the time. "God please let me help this man."

"Corey. I admire your commitment to your relationship to your son. If more boys had a father like you willing to sacrifice to build better relationships, this would be great."

Corey's breathing slowed. "Thanks… I really appreciate that."

"How long does it take your son to fall asleep?"

"At home it takes about 15-20 minutes."

"That's good. I'm making the assumption that after a day of rigorous camping activities the boys will be tired and ready for sleep. Hopefully, you will only need to do this for a short period of time. "

"Okay. I'm listening."

"Set your tent up to so the sleeping bags are facing the tent opening. Unzip the opening to allow fresh air into the tent and allow yourself an opening so you don't fell so claustrophobic. When your son snuggles up next to you to sleep, slightly place your head next to the tent opening and slowly breathe in and out. Take in all the fresh air you can. Focus on the great fun you and your son had during the day, how much you love him, and cherish the moment of time you have now and then."

"What should I do if he doesn't go to sleep but wants to talk?"

"Keep your same position in the tent by the door. Talk with him and tell him one of your favorite Bible stories. Make it adventurous. I have a feeling he will be tired. After he falls asleep, gentle exit the tent and get some more fresh air. Return to the tent. Try going to sleep yourself. At that point your son isn't snuggling up against you."

Corey sighed. "Okay, I'm going to try it. I think it will work. I'm going to try it."

Corey's excursion thousands of miles away in another state brushed through my mind during the weekend at the conference. I wondered how he faired. Late Sunday evening the phone rang. It was Corey.

"How did it go?" There was weeping on the other end of the phone. Oh no!

"Thank you so much for taking the time to help me and share that suggestion. Not only did I survive using your suggestions, it helped me address some of the apprehensions I harbored on being a good father. My son is ecstatic and talking about the camping trip to everyone. I wish you could see the beaming smile on his face. I'm going to talk to my therapist about attending your workshop. I have a feeling it's a place where male survivors of faith can experience the love of Jesus and get some good advice from someone who can relate to the experience."

Pen Action:

- How is sex a bad/good word to you?

- What is your current view of sex?

- What emotion or feelings does a sexual relationship bring up for you?

- Retrace these feelings back to the time when you were abused what do you notice?

- What emotions are associated with the abuse for you?

- If you are single, do you feel that the abuse has affected
- you in such a way that you find it easier to be single?

- If married, do you find it difficult to engage in a sexual relationship with your spouse?

- Do you dissociate or detach yourself during physical intimacy

- List any of the disorders or addictions mentioned above part of your life?

- Have you been sexually abusive to others?

- How comfortable are you discussing this area of the abuse with someone else?

Congratulations! This is a difficult section to really be honest about. If you were not ready to answer the questions, or address the issues, give yourself time. Come back later. Don't get stuck. Keep going. Then return and work on this issue again.

Prayer:

Father, thank you for the opportunity to address some of the issues I'm facing, as I work to heal from abuse. I'm frightened, scared, and confused concerning feelings of intimacy. This is a challenge for me to work through. Please grant me strength.

Please help me find a friend, someone I can trust and confide in, concerning this part of my healing.

> **Truths and promises**
> For whatever is born of God overcomes the world; and this is the victory that has overcome the world – our faith, Who is the one who overcomes the world, but he who believes that Jesus is the Son of God? This is the One who came by water and the blood, Jesus Christ; not with the water only, but with thewater and with the blood. It is the Spirit who testifies, because the Spirit is the turth. *1 John 5:4-6*
>
> Therfore, since we have a great high priest who has passed through the heavens, Jesus the Son of God, let us hold fast our confession. For we do nto have a high priest who cannot sympathize with our weanesses, but One who has been temped in all things as we are, yet without sin. Therefore let us draw near with confidence to the throne of grace sot hat we may receive mercy and find grace to help in time of need. *Hebrews 4:14-16*

Sexuality, Shame and Confusion

Male survivors frequently must deal with confusion concerning their sexuality and masculinity. We mentioned earlier that sex is considered a bad word in many Christian circles. This label often is passed and internalized by the victim. Sex has been labeled as an act of passion. Unfortunately sexual abuse in the minds of many is also labeled in this manner, instead of being viewed as a violent, distorted and destructive crime violation of another person. It is not an act of sexual passion for the victim. Male victims face questions concerning their sexuality. The often unspoken question that we encounter is "What did the sexual abuse do my sexuality or masculinity?" Some of the other question entertained:

Can I function sexually as a man?
Am I man enough?
What do I need to do to prove my manhood?
Does the abuse change my orientation?
Do I have feminine qualities?
Is this why I seem to have same-sex attraction

The function of this book is not to investigate the origin of sexual orientation, gay or heterosexual, but to acknowledge the struggle that sexually abuse men of faith might encounter. I understand this is an explosive topic in the Christian community. It is one of the reasons that we are afraid to help men of faith who have been sexually abuse because the first question or aspect we concern ourselves with is homosexuality, instead of attempting to help the person heal from the sexual abuse. It is a travesty as we are more concerned with labels, stereotypes and outward appearances instead of what's going on inside the heart and soul. The truth is God looks at the heart and man observes the outer appearance. Wish we were more like God. Sexual abuse is mainly not the cause of sexual orientation but constantly leaves the survivor with confused feelings about his sexuality and masculinity. This leads to an even greater problem as all feelings of intimacy are construed to be sexual. Let's put in a context we can all understand. Should a father love his son? Does a father have feelings for his son? He should. Can a man love his male friend? Can he show physical affection toward his father or another man? In our society due the way we have been socialized the language might seem a bit odd because we have Americanized everything in the word that is correct. However, for the sexually abused man even appropriate affectionate feelings toward another man are questioned. Before you read the passages below what would you think if another guy said these words to you? What would be your response?

- There was reclining on Jesus bosom one of His disciples whom Jesus loved. John 12:23
- He leaning back on Jesus bosom said to Him, "Lord, who is it. John 18:25
- He said to Simon Peter, "Simon, do you love me more than these?"
- He said to Him, "Yes LORD, you know that I love you."
- He said to him a second time, "Simon, son of John, Do you love me?"
- He said , "Yes LORD, you know that I love you."
- He said to him the third time, "Simon, son of John, do you love me?"
- Peter was grieved because he said to him the third time, "Do you love me? And he said to Him, "you know everything; you know that I love you." John 21:15-17.
- Love one another with brotherly laffection…Romans 12:10
- Greet one another with a holy kiss. All the churches of Christ greet you. Romans 16:16
- and godliness with brotherly affection, and brotherly affection with love. 2 Peter 1:7

I somewhat chuckle at the interaction between Jesus and Peter placed in a modern day setting. Men can barely say, "I love you" to their spouse☺.

Before we get ballistic and frightened of men displaying brotherly affection for one another let me share a small definition of bosom from a biblical perspective.

> BOSOM Heb ☐êq *refers to the* "under, outer front of [the] human body, where beloved ones, infants [and] animals are pressed"[1]

Yes if we adopted the mainstream American culture and definition of these words many male believers would be running the opposite direction from Jesus afraid that something was awkwardly wrong with Him. Mainly because we allow mainstream culture to redefine the beautiful words and the concepts God has given us to use. For the male survivor to feel such emotions or displays of appropriate affection toward another male might raise a plethora of fears and concerns about his sexuality.

Private words from the heart of one survivor to another
Guys! Questioning your sexuality and masculinity is a

---

[1] Myers, A. C. (1987). *The Eerdmans Bible dictionary* (167). Grand Rapids, Mich.: Eerdmans.

common response to being sexually abused especially if abused by a man. This does not mean you are doomed to become gay. It's important to debunk such myths. It's not a cause and effect scenario. When I have talked with men at the workshops some expressed that the sexual abuse along with other factors may have contributed to their decision to engage and experiment in a homosexual relationship in adulthood, but it was still their decision. Please do not make the mistake of believing myths and lies that if you were sexually abused by a male that homosexuality is a direct response to the abuse. Please do not condemn other male survivors who are struggling with their sexuality and having difficulties in accordance with their faith (Romans 3:23, 1 Corinthians 6:11). If transformation and renewal is to take place, then let God do His work. We can be there to offer support and encouragement.

> A human infant, if left without human touch and interaction will cease to thrive.

Prayer:

Dear Lord, forgive me for the times I doubt you. I'm haunted by memories, feelings and acts committed against me in the past. I wrestle with confusion and fear of not being able to overcome the shame. I struggle with a desire for intimacy in all the wrong ways. Teach me what it means to have true intimacy with others in a way that is pleasing in Your sight. Help me to have faith, and hope while experiencing Your love.

Intimacy

Now before the Feast of the Passover, Jesus knowing that His hour had come that He would depart out of this world to the Father, having loved His own who were in the world, He loved them to the end. *John 13:1*

 Now it came about when he had finished speaking to Saul, that the soul of Jonathan was knit to the soul of David, and Jonathan loved him as himself. *1 Samuel 18:1*

We have been taught that intimacy equates to sex. Contrast this with Jesus. We often consider Him the epitome of manhood. The most masculine man ever, but he lived in intimacy with His disciples. Can you image giving Jesus you a hug? Maybe not, but I think you can understand the closeness the disciples experienced with him. This is what it takes to have that type of **intimacy**:

- Revealing yourself, and becoming vulnerable in a trusting, secure relationship.

- Sharing tenderness, caring, and affection.

- Freely offering and receiving generosity, giving, and sharing.

- Mutual respect with each other.

- Acknowledgement, recognition, and approval of each other's needs.

- A sense of unity with another.

- Demonstration of appropriate physical closeness (like an embrace, handshake, hand on shoulder)

- Proper attitude and esteem of others.

- A sense of distinct bonding with another.

- Understanding brotherly love. (The original word in the Bible was phileo. You may hear Christians use it to distinguish from other forms of love.)

- Understanding of unconditional love. (The original word in the Bible for this is agape.)

Destroyers of Intimacy

In contrast to the intimacy Jesus had with his disciples, these are the things that destroy intimacy:

- Fear of rejection.

- Always on the defensive.

- Power struggles.

- Poor communication.

- Blaming others for problems in the relationship.

- Cannot show affection, tenderness, or caring.

- Cannot be open and honest.

- You deny that you need help.

- Inability to relinquish pain and fears from previous relationships.

- No role models of healthy intimacy.

- Cannot accept your own problem in handling intimacy.

- Fear of being successful in intimacy.

- Cannot accept own responsibility and role to developing intimacy relationships.

- No understanding of handling conflict.

- No development of trust in others.

- A sense of insecurity.

- Fear of failure.

- Fear of being vulnerable.

- Not willing to take a risk.

Abuse and Excitement

Many men are confused or afraid because they felt excitement or pleasure during the sexual abuse. In order to understand this better we need to explore a little biology of the human body and the brain.

Research reports that sex is built into our brains, so it involves body, mind and emotions. As scientists continue to study the brain they are starting to learn that the results of sexual involvements can last a lifetime. In growing, we understand there are transitions physically, emotionally and mentally. Within these transitions we find the emergence of sexual awareness. Perhaps you have seen or experienced the emotional rollercoaster ride during puberty and adolescence for boys as physiological changes with hormones, neurotransmitters, starts the path of sexual awareness. Little electrical storms start lighting up different parts of the brain. An electric storm is initiated when any type of sexual activity or intimate behavior is encountered. Once this brain area is awakened, it's almost impossible to shut it off completely. I think you understand where I'm going with this. Imagine a young child with no context, understanding, knowledge or maturity of sexual behavior being thrust into the awareness of sexuality. It would be like taking a toddler and saying, "You can walk now, you're a man now, go and provide for yourself." The child is not ready. He cannot even feed himself.

Brain research shows, that in non-abusive and unselfish relationships sex begins in the brain as a couple engages in progressive levels of physical contact. As the physical stimulation begins, the areas of the brain light up. This is between consenting adults with the intention of having sexual intercourse. Once again imagine a child being catapulted into this world through abuse. God created sex to be a positive experience, as intimate interaction between two people who care for each other and share their deepest inner feelings for each other. However, misused it can have devastating lifelong negative consequences and effects. Researchers state that "it produces powerful lifelong changes in our brains that direct and influence our future..." Welcome to the world of the sexually abused young boy. In other words, our brains are pliable and our experiences and behaviors can mold our brains.

In your brain

There are many neurotransmitters and chemicals working in the brain from progesterone, testosterone, vasopressin, oxytocin to dopamine. I will not bore you with them all but focus on an important one, dopamine. We know dopamine as the neurotransmitter or chemical that makes you and I feel good when we do something rewarding or exciting. You can imagine the powerful influence this has over human behavior. Dopamine is the reward chemical that floods our brain cells producing the feel-good, well-being and excitement we experience. It also triggers us to feel a need and desire to repeat those rewarding, exciting behaviors. Dopamine produces excitement when catching the winning touchdown, risking opening a business, getting married, having the courage to jump in front of the bullet, having a child, or fixing a problem. The world would not be the same without dopamine. It's part of motivation and well-being and helps influence human behavior. In the context of our conversation there is a crucial key. It is value neutral. It cannot distinguish between right and wrong but is an involuntary response and rewards all kinds of behavior. It rewards the person for healthy or destructive behavior, the rush! Whether it's saving a child, or robbing a bank, you are rewarded with the rush. Taking drugs, excessive drinking, bungee jumping, winner of a marathon, finally completing graduate school, receiving a promotion, reaching your goal, cheating and getting away with it, vengeance and retribution all produce the dopamine reward, the excitement and rush. Notice these behaviors are rewarded whether we interpret them as good or bad. Of course the brain wants more feel good so we are inclined to repeat behaviors that produce the reward chemical. I believe life is about balance.

> Research also shows that adictive drugs like alcohol, cocaine, heroin, nicotine increase dopamine signals. Any exciting behavior triggers the dopamine reward.

You may have probably figured out by now that one of the strongest generators producing the dopamine reward is sex! God's creation made this one of most rewarding and beneficial effects for marriage. Literally the plan would be for a couple to be addicted to sex with each other. Now that's a beautiful picture from the creator. Let introduce another neurochemical called oxytocin. I remember learning about this anatomy and physiology studies. I will not bore you will all the details. We called it the bonding and trust drug. We used to joke that it's the neurochemical that helps women to continue to bond and love men even when they act like jerks. It's present in both genders. The desire to connect is not just emotional but involves physiological initiators as well. Once again these neurochemicals are value neutral. They do not distinguish between, one-time incidents, one night stand, short-term sexual escapade, abusive, non-abusive or lifelong partner for bonding. Like dopamine, oxytocin produces a reward and the brain likes rewards.

With that short biochemical history I hope you can better understand and start fitting the pieces together concerning the sexual abuse. When sexual abuse occurs dopamine is released. There is no "this is right or this is wrong" attached to the neurochemical, just the rush. Now the child who has little or no context and understanding must interpret what has been done to him and what this means. As adults we can barely figure out and understand, nonetheless a child.

Bottom line! Please understand that whether you interpreted the abuse as pleasurable, it still was abuse. The perpetrator was in the wrong and responsible for this, not you. Men who were abused as children must resist the urge to punish themselves because they experienced the normal dopamine, oxytocin reward during the sexually abusive experience. It does not make one homosexual because they experience the dopamine reward while being abused by a male perpetrator. You did nothing wrong. Instead, you were betrayed and mistreated.

I hope that this little section will also illuminate the light bulb in our brains, that perhaps some of the defensive mechanism we use in our life like compulsive disorders, sexual addictions, promiscuity, violent aggressive behavior possible had roots or were generated from our abuse. It's not an excuse for the behavior, but might help us understand where to start probing for answers as we heal. Some men numb themselves from these abusive memories by engaging in compulsive behaviors that become addictive. For example, one workshop participant explained that he would masturbate when he wanted to block out memories of his mother and older brother molesting him when he was nine years old. By looking at beautiful women in Victoria's Secret, he could block out his disgust of the past experience. He said, "I always wanted to believe that I was just a kid who was gifted to be sexually aware at the early age of nine. It took me a long time to both discover and admit that my frequent masturbation--even at age nine or ten--was due to someone making me sexually aware at a very young age. It was easier to accept if I credited myself for discovering sexual pleasure." See how his current behavior which may have started with the dopamine reward abuse as a child, he continues to use as a coping mechanism today. Sex can produce powerful lifelong impacts on the brain. Counselors, pastors, therapists, friends, please show male victims of sexual abuse a little mercy, compassion and understanding when addressing this issue. We need it. Thank you. God Bless.

Let's dig a bit deeper and expand our horizons. To some men this might seem strange or out of place and for others it will loudly resonate. It is rarely discussed and certainly taboo. To utter this thought in faith circles is a death sentence, but it is a reality for some male victims. Therefore I risk further alienation in order to help those that need help, I will discuss.

With all the shame, embarrassment and pain surrounding the sexual abuse, there are instances where the child also felt loved, adored, admired, wanted and the physical contact felt loving. This does not mitigate or lessen the sexual criminal act committed against the boy. The adult still manipulated, coerced and misused the role of power to rape the child. If you resonate with this discussion, you must realize that from the moment you enter this world you have been created with a need for emotional love and connection. For many the attention, admiration of an adult or male figure is prized and welcomed at times. Understanding this deficiency the perpetrator focuses the attention in the form of touching, physical closeness, and sexual contact playing on the basic human need for warmth and closeness. Some of us boys were ripe for the picking. We were deficient, needy, open, vulnerable and naïve. Now as adults we rot inside, seeing ourselves as bad, beating ourselves up because of the emerging feelings of sexuality, closeness, and the security and attention of an older male during our sexual abuse. It causes a lifelong confusion, hurt that only another victim can in its understanding.

Workshop Participants Share

I felt estactic when we were together and he held me. He lavished me with attention that no one else would give me. It was like he was filling an empty hole in my soul. The reality was he was creating a black hole that one day would engulf my very being with darkness. Yet with all the pain I experience today my mind goes back to being loved. That's the only definition of love I had until I came to the workshop. It's starting to change.

At first I resisted. I would get this strange feeling in my stomach. It was like doing a hundred sit-ups. He would ask me do things to him and with him. I'm not sure if he really forced me, but he was patient. Sometimes I felt good inside and it seemed natural. I try not to think about it, but somedays when I'm feeling lonely and socially rejected by other men I find myself thinking about it. Being accepted and loved in this way, eventhough it was rape. Then I feel guilty, embarrassed and depressed.

All touch represents sex to me. Anytime anyone touches me, gives me a compliment I become suspcious, "That person only wants one thing from me, Sex!" I can't turn off the radar. You can imagine how damaging and hurtful this is to any type of relationship. I long for touch, but afraid to risk or pursue it. I learned at the workshop that we were created for loving touch and research shows that infants who are not touched quickly die in a matter of months. I'm dying and I can feel it.

I know this is brief and there is so much more discussion to this section, but that's why we have the workshops. Men have an opportunity to discuss this work through it with a supportive group of guys.

Macho Macho Man

Have you ever pondered this question concerning your trapped state of shame and guilt? "If macho or being manly conveys a sense of daring boldness, why am I afraid to let other people know that I need to be loved?" Imagine the silence this question generates at our workshops.

Some once shared with me a lecture from Dr. Henry Cloud's on the importance of asking for love.

- **Asking for help develops humility.** "Lord's it hard to be humble when you're hurting in every way…I can't wait to deny all the feelings, they only get worse each day..." becomes our adapted theme song. I'm beating myself up on my own mistakes. I personally must confess that self-sufficiency used to be my god , idol (Baal) of my life in dealing with CSA.

-
- **Asking shows we own our needs.** It's a polite way to not demand but take responsibility for our needs. By asking you are ad-mitting you have a need, without expecting, forcing or obligating a response from another. This provides the other person the choice and freedom to connect with you without obligation.
-
- **Asking demonstrates initiative.** Don't force people to be mind readers. You can wish that someone will help you or sense your pain, but you only have desire without any expectation and that leads to further disappointment and hurt. By asking we demonstrate a level of control.
-
- **Asking develops a character of gratefulness.** (Luke 7:47)
- **Asking increases your chances of actually getting help.** We have all familiar with the biblical principle "Ask and you shall receive...If you ask enough times you might actually obtain the assistance you desire.

Pen Action:

- Where you sexually abused by a male or female?

- How do you feel this has affected your identity as being a man?

- How was your perspective of masculinity affected?

- Were you confused with sexual identity as a result?

- Do you currently feel conflicted in your sexual identity?

- How has the abuse affected your view of homosexuality?

- How do you over compensate or under compensate in your views of homosexuality to get past the shame, embarrassment, or guilt of the abuse?

- If you were abused by a female, what was her relationship to you?

- How has your abuse affected your view towards women?

- How has your abuse affected your view towards men?

- How do you treat or approach men or women differently based on the abuse you experienced?

- Are you afraid that the sexual abuse felt pleasurable at some point

- If it felt exciting or pleasurable, do you believe that it wasn't abuse?

- How do perceive this heinous crime committed against

- you although it might have felt pleasurable?

- How difficult is this subject matter for you to share with another?

- Is this a subject you could discuss at a survivor workshop, with a counselor, therapist, or safe friend?

Congratulations again! This is one of the most difficult sections to be honest about. If you were not able or ready to answer the questions, or address the issues, give yourself time. Come back later. Then return and work on this issue again.

Let me share: This is always one of the most difficult sessions for me. There are times in my life when I must revisit these questions in my life. An event, picture thought, words or sound triggers memories and produce feelings that must be addressed again. The pain is less intense and the duration shorter, but still a lifelong process.

Prayer:

Lord, this addresses some core issues in me. I feel angry and resentful because my current bad identity has been forced upon me. I didn't make the choice, but struggle because of someone's selfishness. Lord I need help. I need you to remind me that I am a child of God. This is my first identity. I need to claim your promise that I can do all things through Jesus who gives strength. Lord, I need friends who can I honestly trust and share this with, to help me start healing this area of my life. I'm scared, embarrassed and feel shameful. Please help me to find assistance and a friend.

Truths and Promises

Trust in the LORD with all your heart and do nto lean on your own understanding. In all your ways acknowledge Him, and He will make your paths straight. Do not be wise in yoru own eyes; Fear the LORD and turn away from evil. It will be healing to you. *Proverbs 3:5-8*

Manly Images

Another difficulty arises from balancing the manhood puzzle. From Superman, Batman, John Wayne, Green lantern to James Bond, American culture has offered us heroes to emulate. From earliest childhood, these images are instilled and they shaped our desires, passions, and behaviors as a man. Somewhere you were exposed to various patterns and actions that helped form your beliefs of manhood. Our literature, media does not create, but reflects our cultural attitudes. As young boys grow, they watch listen and mimic the behavior of adult males. We transmit our values, culture, ideas, and norms. Boys who do not fit those acceptable behaviors suffer negative consequences. Every socieity has their cultural norms. If you had to draw a picture of the ideal successful American man he would be independent, tough, powerful, rich, physically strong, aggressive, handsome, self-sufficient, ladies man, can protect himself, accomplished, into sports, risk-taker, competitive, dominant, and in control. We are often socialized to believe that anything less is an anomaly. This is what it means to be male.

For instance, how does a man receive recognition in today's world? Success! What does success look like? If you believe the culturally ideal images, a man is always a take-charge kind of guy, aggressive and assertive, and decisive. He has a great corporate job. He is wealthy and accomplished and has a nice home. He knows how to talk to the ladies. He is muscular, handsome, and exudes confidence. He is famous, and gregarious. Society rewards those who fit this image. Movie stars and politicians are among those who exude wealth and fame, and fit the pop culture ideal of success.

What boy didn't want to grow up to be a man like this? Each year we compared ourselves to these guys. We couldn't wait to have our own set of wheels, money, and a girlfriend. Later we wanted an important job, prestige, and more money. The puzzle pieces do not always fit together for sexual abuse victims, because the earliest childhood images instilled are not part of the accepted picture. We are baffled and confused because we are do fit this ideal mold of manhood.

The desire to become a so-called "real man" became frustrated when we were violated. We did not dominate, but were forced into submission. We were compliant in order to survive.. Compliancy is viewed as passivity. Passivity is directly opposed to the take-charge man we are to represent, and we fail to fit the socialized expectation of manliness. We end up feeling worthless because we accept this rigid view masculinity. For example which of these characteristics are considered masculine: strong, assertive, seductive, emotional, tough, vulnerable, reckless, nurturing, tender, competitive, sympathetic, affectionate, sensitive, confident, competent, good listener, intuitive, instinctive, playful. The ones we often pick as feminine are, emotional, tender, intuitive, affectionate, sensitive, sympathethic, nurturing. Funny how those characteristics we consider feminine were the characteristics of the greatest biblical figure and man on whom are faith is founded, Jesus. How are we defining masculinity? Or whose definition matters?

The reality is that male survivors often view themselves throung the glasses of socio-cultural male stereotypes. We would have different expectations of ourselves than female survivors. Don't get me wrong, I am not a proponent that men and women don't have differences, I believe they do and part of that difference is socially learned. However when it comes to ideal characteristics like the dopamine, they are neutral. Can men be nurturing? Yes. We might display it differently, but it's still nurturing. Both genders are born with the full capacity to express the gamat of emotions in this human condition. Many men and survivors are stunted in their personal growth as they accept the socio-cultural male stereotypes. For some reason there is a gap in the expectation of sexuality for men versus women. In the sexual arena men are expected to be sexually aggressive, dominant, experienced, easily aroused, knowledgeable and confident. Women are expected to be coy, shy, virgins, timid, submissive, passive and inexperienced by societal norms. What is to be said of the male who has been sexually dominated or subjected, who is passive, not confident and passive. Our society relegates such men to third-class citizen neutered manhood status. Sometimes I wonder how the biblical character Joseph would fit into our stereotypes today as a man running away from a woman attempting to seduce him. Are you sure something isn't wrong with him?

Why do feel worthless? Besides the obvious reason of not conforming to the manly stereotypes, we have a need that we have been taught only has one definition. Intimacy means sex. Let me regress a bit.

Intimacy, the need to be close and loved has only one definition for men, sex. For example, try using the term intimate in the same sentence concerning a male friend. "John, my life-long best friend and I have an intimate friendship" Write me and tell me the feedback you received. Why does this sentence sound wierd? It is because we often equate intimacy with sexual activity or sexual intimacy. When in reality intimacy is based on relationship with others, not ourselves. We have been taught that men are to be self-sufficient conquerors, independent rugged mountain men. This is a half truth. The true mark of manhood is built upon his relationships with others. Think about it. If you lived on a deserted island, how would your manhood be expressed? Would it be expressed by the number of fish you caught, the number of coconuts you gathered, or the size of your mud hut? Who would care? Our society fails to focus on real marks of manly character. Will you be a man of your word? Are you kind and trustworthy? Where do you have opportunity to display character? Character is displayed in our relationships with others.

Are Men Always Strong

Joshua was the strong and courageous warrior, the captain of the army of the Lord. He warred and defeated nations. He had testosterone. He was a real man, and had real masculinity. He was an ancient John Wayne. However, when reading his story, we run into a different picture. God said to him, Have I not commanded you? Be strong and courageous! Do not tremble or be dismayed, for the Lord your God is with you wherever you go. (Joshua 1:9)"

This was the third time that God told Joshua to be strong! Have you ever thought about that? Why would God need to reaffirm this courageous leader of men three times? Or what about the boisterous, impetuous Peter who swears his dying allegiance to defend and protect Jesus? He cowered to the meager statements of some servant girl, "You too are one of them". Peter cursed and swore then, "I do not know the man!" (Matthew 26:69).

Joshua and Peter were real men, but they made mistakes. They were human, made of dust also. They had times of frailty, doubt, and fear. We Christian men who were victims of childhood sexual abuse can learn from them. Jesus has provided us with the grace to help those who are in need. As men healing from this abuse, we must have courage to seek this help.

Ed's Shares

I figured that when I was married the addictions and pornography would go away. I have been working on these things, reading and memorizing scripture, and changing my behavior, but the problems would always seem to rear their ugly heads.

A close friend noticed my predicament. He offered to share his experience with similar issues. Our conversations were like verbal judo. He seemed to know exactly what to listen for, and asked a few thought provoking questions concerning my family and childhood. It was almost like he was reading my mind. It was uncanny.

Before I knew it, the tears were flowing from my eyes, and I was crying like a child. I do not remember ever being molested as a child. I just remember that my sexual behavior started around age seven, which is really early for a child…

This hurts too much and I can't deal with it now. I know my friend only wants to help me, but it's too much emotion and pain. I have to shut him down. No more talking about this stuff. I can't have him or others seeing me like this. Deep inside of me, I have a feeling something is true, but if I face it, I feel my world may crumble around me."

Struggling Masculinity

If there is one aspect many CSA male survivors struggle with it's in the arena of masculinity. There is often a struggle to reconcile the sexual abuse with visions of what it means to be a man. There are two major obstacles areas where our masculinity is compromised (1) self-perception (2) socially constructed ideal of being a man.

Let's delve a little bit into our psychology or thoughts. As men who were raped and sexually abused as boys we face some challenging issues. By even mentioning the word abuse interferes with viewing ourselves as normal. Men are expected to be able to protect themselves. When we as survivors admit or disclose the circumstances in which we were abused and unable to protect ourselves, we feel like we have denied our masculinity. Often guys will say to me, "But I didn't stop it! I should have said no! Why didn't I scream or yell? There-fore, I allowed it to hap-pen." The reality that fear, confusion and betrayal are petrifying doesn't resonate in our minds as adults like it did as boys.

The key word here is "feel". That is our self-perception. We often forget the power differential associated with sexual abuse and view our masculinity as weak and vulnerable. We begin to perpetuate this myth and find it difficult to build healthy relationships with other guys feeling like we are less of a man. But where does our self-perception of masculinity come from? We learn it through family, friends, media and other sources. We have influences from everywhere defining masculinity: Real men

- Don't cry!
- Are sexually promiscuous
- Are not sexually abused
- Are not vulnerable
- Are always strong
- Never display emotion that is out of control

Can I be frank here? I'm so glad that I'm a Christian and the best example I have of masculinity is the perfect man, Jesus. Without his example, I might believe a lot of the garbage that society dictates as norms. How do we break this self-perception? One avenue is to find and build healthy male relationships where true character is lived. What do I mean by that?

Do you think that Jesus had a masculinity problem? Most believers would say no. It wasn't his masculinity that defined him, it was his character. Character has nothing to do with gender. As we are working through the issues of being masculine it's important to focus on character. Did Jesus cry? Did he allow his emotion to be seen? Was he ever in agony? Did people mistreat and hurt him? Did people take advantage and try to use him? Yes, Yes, Yes! Did this make him any less masculine? No. He always responded with character. We are not discounting the reality that we may feel less manly at times as survivors of sexual abuse, we are simply attempting to change our perception and acknowledge a bit of truth in adjusting our thinking so we can work through the issues.

Pen Action:

Explain how men can be victims?

Do you view yourself as a victim of childhood sexual abuse?

How do you believe being a victim makes you less masculine?

Do you consider yourself as a survivor of childhood sexual abuse?

Name several of your heroes and people you admire: _

Why do you admire them?

Have you ever had an opportunity to see your hero cry or hurt?

How did that effect your perception of that person's strength?

What do you think about Jesus weeping, Joseph crying? Was that masculine?

Describe the man you are and want to be:

Describe the man you believe you are expected to be by people:

Do you believe God can supply you the strength to overcome the wrong you have
suffered?

Describe the man you believe God wants you to be:

> **Truths and Promises**
>
> Behold, I stand at the door and knowck; if anyone hears My voice and opens the door, I will come in to him and will dine with him, and he with Me. *Revelation 3:10*
>
> Consider it all joy, my brethern, when you encounter various trials, knowing that the testing of your faithproduces endurance. *James 1:2-3*
>
> And without faith it is impossible to please Him, for he who comes to God must believe that He is and that He is a rewarder of those who seek Him. *Hebrews 11:6*

Here is a story that was shared with me.

Losing a Contact Lens

A friend of mine name Brenda told me a true story about rock climbing. In spite of her fear, she put on the gear, took a hold on the rope, and started up the face of a granite cliff. She got to a ledge where she could take a breather. As she was hanging on there, the safety rope snapped against Brenda's eye and knocked out her contact lens.

Well, there she was on a rock ledge, nothing but air hundreds of feet below her or above her. Of course, she looked and looked on the ledge, hoping the contact had landed there, but it was gone.

Here she was, far from home, her sight now blurry. She was desperate, and began to get upset. So she prayed to the Lord to help her to find it.

When she got to the top of the cliff, a friend examined her eye and her clothing for the lens, but the contact lens was to be found. She sat down, despondent, waiting for the rest of the group to make it up. She looked out across range after range of mountains, thinking of that Bible verse that says, "The eyes of the Lord run to and fro throughout the whole earth." She thought, Lord, You can see all these mountains. You know every stone and leaf, and You know exactly where my contact lens is. Please help me.

Finally, they walked down the trail to the bottom. Another party of climbers had just started up the face of the cliff. One of them shouted out, "Hey, you guys! Anybody lose a contact lens?"

Well, that was startling enough, but do you know how the climber saw the lens? An ant was moving slowly across the face of the rock, carrying it.

Brenda's father is a cartoonist. When she told him the incredible story of the ant, the prayer, and the contact lens, he drew a picture of an ant lugging that contact lens. The ant said, "Lord, I don't know why You want me to carry this thing. I can't eat it, and it's awfully heavy. But if this is what You want me to do, I'll carry it for You."

I think it would do of us good to occasionally say, "God, I don't know why you want me to carry this load. I can see no good in it and it's awfully heavy. But, if you want me to carry it, I will."

God can bring ordinary people through some extraordinary things.

What I have learned…

- ..That trying to do this alone is impossible. No matter how embarrassing it may seem to solicit the help of others, they are needed. God created us to be interdependent with each other and when we disregard that principle we suffer.

- ..That when the relationship is unilateral you must let the other person go, no matter how much you want to be a part of their life.

- ..That there are bucket fillers and bucket drainers in life. Or perhaps vampire is a better word because they suck all the life out of you and never fill or give anything in return. If you are doing all the emailing, calling, hosting, keeping in touch, you're in a relationship by yourself. Find someone else who cares and shows it!

Take a Break!

Before you continue, stop! Take a walk. Breathe deeply as you walk. Walk for about 15-20 minutes through a park or forest. Enjoy the natural beauty around you. Think about how blessed you are to be finally working through some of the issues. Take a couple of days, weeks whatever you need, to process your journey up to this point.

Pen Action: Take some time to journal what you are experiencing right now.

Chapter Six
Healing

And looking at them Jesus said to them, "With people this is impossible, but with God all things are possible." Matthew 19:26

> HEALING: alleviate, improve, make healthy, renew, repair, harmonize, ameliorate, revive, correct recover, remedy, wholesome, recuperate.

You are filled with a little hope, but you are scared out of your wits. Is healing really possible or is this all a charade? You would like to get rid of this ball and chain however, the thought of being open and working through feelings and memories prompts fear and erases what little hope you possess. What does healing mean? What does it look like? Do you have to take the elevator to the highest building walk out on the balcony and scream to the world, "I am a survivor of childhood sexual abuse!" Or setup an appointment with a therapist, have a few sessions, talk about it with a friend. You feel somewhat paranoid, not from a psychological you have lost your mind perspective, but wondering who is safe and who is not. Who can you trust and will they be able to help you? You want to believe the lie that many believers recite. "You only need God and that's it!" He will take care of all your problems. Yet deep down you know that God calls us into relationship and connection and healthy healing does not take place in isolation, but you wish it did. You've been to celebrate recovery meetings and they seem like a novel idea, but your subject just doesn't seem to get covered in a way that is helpful. You know that it's a wonderful outreach. You have worked through a few of the sections of this book and have identified individuals you believe are safe, but cannot muster the courage to start the conversation. Your fiancee loves you but the emotional vomiting about this issue is beginning to strain the relationship and she cannot bear much more. Would you be better if

A friend is someone who can see the truth and pain in you even when you are fooling everyone else.
- Unknown -

you confronted your abuser? Is part of healing finally getting closure by confronting and hearing the answer to "Why did you abuse me?"

To Tell

Let's start with an obvious part of healing. You must tell someone. That really not the difficult portion. I found that deciding what I was going tell presented the greatest challenge. How much detail did I need to give? What would they think about me? When shattering the silence for the first time, it's helpful to set some expectations for yourself by saying , „" if you could just listen to what I have say, no questions, advice or problem-solving right now, just listening would be helpful" can be quite effective. This just depends on how comfortable you are with the individual. Time and place are also important. Christmas or Thanksgiving gatherings might not be the appropiate time or place. One survivor at the workshop shared how he shared at the Thanksgiving table how his grandfather had sexually abused him. You don't have to imagine how thanksgiving ended. Not saying that he was wrong for finally disclosing, however he was not prepared for the backlashing and vitrial he received from the family. It literally almost killed him.

As you attempt to throw off the shackles and discover truth, numerous issues will hold you back. Unfortunately in the secular world and in the Christian community, men surviving sexual abuse issues are often ignored. I don't believe that Christians intentionally mean to be cold and unresponsive, but we definitely are negligent. Our negligence is steeped in fear, ignorance and the discomfort of dealing with such taboo subjects. As male survivors often we contemplate, "Why do I need to address this? Can I just ignore it? Will it resolve itself over time?" This attitude often is derived from a place of fear and embarrassment. Numerous men live with the secret of being sexually, physically and emotional abused. No one wants to feel vulnerable especially in a society where men have been socialized to reject any notions of being a victim. It's scary! However, the traumatic pain and stress of the abuse buried in the subconscious often produces long-term consequences and sequelae. No matter how much we attempt to ignore it affects our everyday life, relationships with God, the wife, the kids, the family, friends, and ourselves. There is a general consensus in literature that CSA also can result in long-term mental health issues for men. Specific effects relating to men include shame, guilt, extreme anger, masculine identity, withdrawal, suppression, substance abuse, suicidal tendencies, compulisve addictions, unhealthy aggression and more. Although men usually do not report significant effects when later diagnosed many of them actually meet the criteria for posttraumatic stress disorder (PTSD) compared to men not abused. Would it be correct to assume that you would give anything to lessen the burden? I believe there is hope and help. Breaking free will require Jesus' love, God's word, a trusting attitude, psychological insight, social and emotional support, and the capability to be vulnerable..

Why not Isolation?

The biblical principle of isolation being detrimental is real. Research has also shown that men who are willing to receive social and emotional support from activities like workshops, survivor groups, counseling are more likely to adopt positive coping strategies which lead to better psychological and emotional adjustment. Some men are afraid to start the process. Others decided to rebury the pain after they start because they are embarrassed by the expression of emotions.

> He who isolates himself seeks his own desire; He breaks out against all sound judgment. Proverbs 18:1 (ESV)

Pen Action: Write the areas of your life that are being affected by the past abuse.

Prayer:

Father I truly have a need to heal from the hurt, shame and embarrassment of my abuse. Please give me the strength to not ignore Your wisdom and healing power. Help me to not be comfortable with isolation and settle for life in its current state. I am scared! It is difficult to trust things I cannot see and things I do not understand. Increase my faith in You and help me to allow others who are trustworthy to help me. Lord it is about what you can do through me. Let me be open to allow this painful healing to begin. Help me to remember your faithfulness and allow me to be victorious. Please reign in me.

Truths and Promises

It is a trustworthy statement
For if we died with Him, we will also live with Him;
If we endure, we will also reign with Him;
If we deny Him, He also will deny us;
2 Timothy 2:22-12

Transforming the Worst to the Best

When they came to Marah, they could not drink the waters of Marah, for they were bitter; therefore it was named Marah. So the people grumbled at Moses, saying, "What shall we drink?" Then he cried out to the LORD, and the LORD showed him a tree; and he threw it into the waters, and the waters became sweet. There He made for them a statute and regulation, and there He tested them. Exodus 15:23-25 (NASB)

God truly can provide healing for the bitter experiences of life. In order to claim the healing we must not follow the example of the Israelites. They murmured and complained. We must trust and pray that God's love always works in our best interest.

Healing Takes Time

Healing often progresses in stages. A deep cut does not heal overnight; it goes through stages of healing. A scab forms and crusts over the wound to provide surface protection, similar to a Band-Aid. Underneath the body attends to the infection within. As that healing continues, the scab slowly sheds because it's less needed for protection. The gaping wound becomes a scar. Healing from sexual and emotional abuse is similar. Using defensive mechanisms like fantasy and rationalization protects the child temporarily until he reaches adulthood, if the issues have not been dealt with and worked through, they fester and wreak havoc in the man's life. What needs to be done?

The painful issues of the abuse must be exposed, so healing can begin. The healing balms of loving Christian support, God's word, counseling/therapy and practical principles are essential. Remember, you and others will need the patience as you deal with many of these issues. Here's another illustration.

A man's car stalled in the heavy traffic as the light turned green. All his efforts to start the engine failed, and a chorus of honking cars behind him only made matters worse. He finally got out of his car and walked back to the first driver and said, "I'm sorry, but I can't seem to get my car started. If you'll go up there and give it a try, I'll stay here and blow the horn for you."

You will need to be patience with others and yourself. Often I have heard Christians express frustration at the progress of hurting men struggle with abuse issues. "Why doesn't he get over it? Like yesterday!" When others are behind you honking their horns for a speedy recovery be patient. Share the car illustration. Be patient, deep wounds require work and time to heal.

Henry Shares

Henry shared his story at the workshop. I am honored to share the story he wrote and read.

"Sharing and breaking the secret of my abuse has been a powerful, active force in dealing with my brokenness. But before I do, let me tell you that being this transparent, honest and open is very frightening for me. Exposing the secret means that some of you will not like me or accept me. When you meet me, you will no longer be able to view me as a person, but as damaged goods, tainted by crimes and sins of another, and stuck with the stigma of abuse.

"Real change happens, when the pain of staying the same is greater than the pain of changing."
- Sheldon Kopp -

Some of you will avoid me. You won't talk to me. Some will believe that I have a creative imagination. They believe such abuses are not possible in a Christian home, where God is supposed to reign. They will brand me as a creative thinker or liar. Some of you feel uncomfortable because you have similar issues conveniently tucked away in the recesses of your mind. My story really bothers you, because deep inside your heart, you know that something horrible has happened to you also, but you are afraid to admit it. I say these things because when I started facing the demons in my life, these kinds of thoughts breathed life into the power of secrecy. My perpetrators had said, "If you tell what happened, people will think you are strange. They will not like you. They will abandon you. Your parents will blame you. Your mom will freak out. People will think you are gay. They will not believe you. So this is our secret, Okay?" They were right.

The power that this secrecy holds over me today is amazing. I have experienced these reactions from sharing my story, and each time reminds me of being a helpless child that no one will hear and protect. I remember the power and control my abusers had over me. Today I will ignore what others think of me. I will break free from the shackles of secrecy and share with you, so we can begin to heal.

My dad used to get very angry. Today people call it an "anger management problem". That sounds like a nice, politically correct way to mask the truth that he was like Darth Vader. He made a covenant with his dark side, and released his rage on me. Some of the memories are vivid with color, smells, feelings and emotions that sometimes still get triggered today. It's ironic. The mind seems to have an endless capacity to retain life experiences, and no matter how much we strive to block out bad memories, they show up in our life, until we face them. The scent of beer and stench of urine triggers vivid memories. Public restrooms at sporting events are not my favorite places.

Everyone cleared space when the bottle uninhibited Dad's rage. When car door slammed, I knew what to expect. When he violated me, I felt serious discomfort when I froze or tightened my body from the shock, but I learned to relax. After a while I learned to mentally transport myself to worlds unknown. When he was finished, he would clean me up. It was as if he realized his crimes and felt remorse. Strangely enough, I felt there was something in my father I wanted to connect with. He had an affectionate side he never showed at other times, and I wanted access to it.

Adulthood has brought many challenges. I had totally repressed any of my childhood memories. Memories from age eight to thirteen were lost. However, the manifestation of them in my life was obvious. I never really trusted anyone, especially father figures. I heard that God was my heavenly father figure, but as far as I was concerned, all fathers were like dad. How could I develop any real bonding male relationships?

The blow of rejection by those in my family, and Christians I considered to be my friends devastated me. They said, "Why bring that up know? That was years ago! You just have to live with it and get over it!" I am damaged goods. No one wanted to deal with the sexual abuse because they were afraid of me.

They were afraid of the subject, and they felt inept to deal with it. I felt alone. My freedom began when God blessed my life with a church member who listened. He didn't run from my story. He listened to me. I didn't see shock or disgust on his face as I shared some of the gory details. No strange winces or grimaces. He has been so instrumental in helping me start the healing of my brokenness. I hope my openness today will help others."

Recovery Is Real but You Need Help

In the Christian community, healing and recovery from childhood sexual abuse and victimization is challenging. We often make it more challenging by feeding on clichés. How many times have survivors been told "Just read these scriptures and pray! Everything will work out and God will heal you." This type of response reminds me of

> And one of you says to them, "Go in peace, be warmed and be filled," and yet you do not give them what is necessary for their body, what use is that? *James 2:16*

We often overlook the crucial help of others in the healing process. Have you ever thought about how wonderfully complicated human beings are? God has created us to be awesomely complex, to the point that we need more than just

Him alone. Okay, before you throw this book in the garbage can for blasphemy, consider this.

When He created God said, "It's not good for man to be alone." Adam existed in the perfect paradise garden with God; he had no sin, disease, hunger, or problems. What more could a man ask for? Yet God understood that because of the way He had created Adam, the man needed human contact, human help, and human interaction. God had created a man with a spiritual aspect that only God could fill, but he created another part that needed emotional and social support with another of his kind. What an awesome God, who unselfishly does not hog everything!

My adoptive father once taught me that true security and significance comes from God. When trusting in God, a person can never be taken away. Yet, in the relationships God has blessed us with, God also provides a level of security and significance. It's our job to help others by encouraging them, supporting them, and lifting them up. We don't merely seek our own interest, but bear one another's burdens, and restore those who are trapped. We help with a spirit of gentleness. So how does this relate to the healing process of male sexual abuse? Our Christian family and friends need to be part of the solution, the answered prayer. We need to allow them the opportunity to love and help us. Understand that everyone will not have the ability to minister or serve in this capacity. Dealing with men who have been sexually victimized as children brings a gamut of issues, but a Christian friend doesn't have to hold a Ph.D. in Clinical Psychology to have compassion. The kind of compassion I'm talking about moves a one to give you a book on the subject, to financially help you attend a workshop, or just mention the fact he cares and takes the time to listen.

Pen Action:

- Do you feel embarrassed, shameful about your sexual abuse?

- Do you believe you can handle these issues yourself?

- Does your abuse feel more sinister because the gender of the perpetrator?

- How do you think others fill respond toyour abuse story?

- What attitude will church members have toward sexually abused men?

- Do you know of members who can help you during this process?

Facing Feelings

Facing the feelings surrounding your sexual abuse is probably one the most difficult aspects of the healing process. At first it seems daunting and you feel dread and apprehensive, but as you learn to express and communicate your feelings in an effective way the intensity often slowly subsides. As men we believe that logic and cognitive prowess will release us from the pain, but it is the balance of feeling and thinking that liberates us. Balance simply means having the ability to identify and communicate your feelings surrounding the abuse.

As children, we frequently attempted to protect ourselves from emotional pain of the abuse by cloaking our feelings. We did not cry out, we held it in. Why did we do that? Was this a conscious or subconscious reaction? There are many reasons, it's much easier to deny than to face the possibility of rejection or more harm. One workshop participant reported that during incidents of his sexual abuse he discovered that when he expressed emotions by crying or screaming his father became angered and abused him more often and harder. He learned it was advantageous to keep quiet and suffocate his own feelings. Today he struggles in his marriage and family relationships. He views expression of emotion, feelings as weak and unnecessary. Crying kids or an expressive wife during arguments are ticking time bombs. He tries his best to keep the anger in check, but his own unresolved abuse issues often skew his vision. Catch twenty-two! He blows up in anger, but views expression of feelings as weak, therefore logically in his mind he's worthless.

Workshop Participants Share

"It took a while for me to remember what had happened, but when it did it devastated me. They say the honeymoon is a time of discovery. It is. The moment I became physically intimate with my new bride. I freaked. The way she touched me awoke a nightmare that had been dormant for fifteen years. God only knows how much I emotionally damaged her, but I just couldn't handle it. Each time we engaged in sexual intimacy, I felt nauseauous, suffocated, I panicked and grew distant." "When you learn that much of the crap in your life has been related in some way to your sexual abuse it hurts. The man who I trusted and called friend hurt me forever. I remembered or realized I had been sexually assaulted only a couple of years ago. Some days it was easy to say, „"This happened to me!" Other times I would willingly return to my mental slumber to keep from dealing it it, numbing myself, which made it a thousand times worse."

Why are there effects long-term? Often because we have unresolved issues in the form of feelings. I remember sitting in graduate school and my psychology professor expousing his counseling principle dealing with fealings. "Feelings do not have time parameters. Those feelings that you did or not express in the past, are still there to be expressed in the present and the future. Often we are experiencing today, the feelings we did not or could not express then. " Confronting and experiencing those feelings are crucial to healing. There is no need to fear feelings because they simply are physical and psychological reactions to events that affect us. We call them feelings because to some degree they are something we feel in our body. It not just intellectual. We are fearfully and wonderfully made!

Vocabulary to Express Feelings

One of the issues we often experience is a limited vocabulary of feeling words. It becomes difficult identify feelings attached to the sexual abuse if we do not have the vocabulary to express them. Consider the list below as you begin to discover. Set of feeling words

Levels of Intensity		HAPPY		
Strong	Excited	Ecstatic	Energized	Thrilled
	Elated	Terrific	Enthusiastic	Uplifted
	Exuberant	Jubilant	Loved	Marvelous
Mild	Justified	Joyful	Grateful	Accepted
	Resolved	Proud	Appreciated	Amused
	Valued	Cheerful	Confident	Delighted
	Encouraged	Assured	Admired	Fulfilled
	Optimistic	Determined		
	Tranquil	Glad	Peaceful	Pleased
	Content	Good	Hopeful	Flattered
	Relaxed	Satisfied	Fortunate	

---

[1] http://www.brighterdays4you.com/Feeling.htm

SCARED

Strong	Fearful	Terrified	Appalled	Overwhelmed
	Panicky	Intimidated	Vulnerable	Dread
	Afraid	Desperate	Horrified	Tormented
	Shocked	Frantic	Petrified	
Mild	Tense	Insecure	Alarmed	Guarded
	Threatened	Skeptical	Shaken	Stunned
	Uneasy	Swamped	Awed	Apprehensive
	Defensive	Suspicious	Startled	
Weak	Reluctant	Shy	Timid	Perplexed
	Anxious	Nervous	Concerned	Doubtful
	Impatient	Unsure		

CONFUSED

Strong	Bewildered	Directionless	Baffled	Immobilized
	Trapped	Stagnant	Flustered	Constricted
Mild	Foggy	Torn	Ambivalent	Misunderstood
	Perplexed	Doubtful	Awkward	Disorganized
	Hesitant	Troubled	Puzzled	

	Surprised	Distracted	Unsure	Uncomfortable
	Unsettled	Bothered	Uncertain	Undecided

SAD

Strong	Devastated	Exhausted	Empty	Terrible
	Hopeless	Helpless	Miserable	Unwanted
	Sorrowful	Crushed	Distraught	Unloved
	Depressed	Worthless	Deserted	Mournful
	Wounded	Uncared for	Grievous	Pitiful
	Hurt	Dejected	Burdened	Discarded
	Drained	Rejected	Demoralized	Disgraced
	Defeated	Humbled	Condemned	
Mild	Lonely	Resigned	Disheartened	Unappreciated
	Neglected	Drained	Despised	Discouraged
	Isolated	Slighted	Disappointed	Ashamed
	Alienated	Degraded	Upset	Distressed
	Abandoned	Deprived	Inadequate	Distant
	Regretful	Wasted	Dismal	Disillusioned
	Hated			
Weak	Sorry	Bad	Deflated	Disturbed

Lost   Apathetic   Disenchanted

ANGRYs

Strong				
	Strangled	Abused	Rebellious	Mad
	Furious	Hateful	Pissed Off	Spiteful
	Seething	Humiliated	Outraged	Patronized
	Enraged	Sabotaged	Fuming	Vindictive
	Hostile	Betrayed	Exploited	Used
	Vengeful	Repulsed	Throttled	Incensed

Mild	Ridiculed	Offended	Irritated	Perturbed
	Resentful	Exasperated	Infantilized	Provoked
	Disgusted	Controlled	Harassed	Dominated
	Smothered	Peeved	Anguished	Coerced
	Frustrated	Annoyed	Deceived	Cheated
	Stifled	Agitated	Aggravated	
Weak	Uptight	Dismayed	Tolerant	Displeased

Pen Action: Highlight or circle any words above that express feelings you experience(d) concerning your sexual abuse. Then write in the space provided below.

Prayer:

God, I'm not sure that I'm yet ready to share my abuse with others yet. I'm really scared. Father, I ask for friends that I can trust and open my heart to. When the time comes, help me accept the assistance of others who love me and desire to support me. Help me remember that no one is perfect, and they will do their best. Help me to remember that we are all but dust.

> **Truths and Promises**
>
> It's important to remember that it wasn't the hem of Jesus' garment or His clothes that contained the power, but Jesus himself. When we pray for help during our times of struggle, it is not the eloquent prayer that fills the request. The request is filled because Jesus has the power to answer the prayer. *Luke 6:19*

Anger A Quick Note

Anger has been demonized in many faith circles. It's a God given emotion that we not only experience, but have biblical authority to "be angry and sin not" when kept in proper righteous parameters. Anger is a powerful emotion that humans experience. It is an emotion that you will probably experience at some point along the healing path. Countless number of men participant in the workshop and utter these words, "I'm so angry and I just don't know where it comes from?" If we are going to work through the issues it's important to recognize where it comes from so we can communicate it.

This emotion is a common reaction for survivors. It represents the feelings you have toward being violated by a trusted individual.

Everyone doesn't agree with this statement I'm about to make, but I'm sharing my own personal experience and work with other men. Feeling angry is necessary for healing. I have seen numerous men emotionally, intellectually and psychologically destroyed because they lived with unresolved anger instead of expressing it and working through the issues. Fortunately, in the world of male socialization it is the one emotion we are allowed to experience without so much negativity associated compared to crying because we are sad.

Building up Defenses

A brother offended is harder to be won than a strong city, and contentions are like the bars of a citadel. Proverbs 18:19

We were resilient as children, whether we realized it or not. To deal with our abuse, we learned to build up defenses to protect our hearts and minds. We didn't know the big fancy names given to these defensive mechanisms. Unfortunately, we have adamantly clung to some of these detrimental defenses and carried them into adulthood. Here's a quick lesson in psychological terms. I want to share with you some of the defensive mechanisms I learned that may help you to better understand and identify.

Displacement. One way to ignore the feelings and emotions tied to our experience is to displace them, moving them from one area to another, so we don't have to deal with them. Or we put the emotions somewhere other than where they rightfully belong. For example, if you show anger at your supervisor, you might lose your job. So you redirect it. When you get home, you pick a fight with your wife. Or you kick the dog.

Sublimation. Instead of negatively displacing emotion, sublimation is the healthy redirection. There were times when I felt like beating my abusers to a pulp . Instead of punching them, I used martial arts against a punching bag. Some people redirect by becoming champions for children's rights.

Projection. Projection is something everyone does. Think of a movie being projected from the inside of the camera to the screen, and you have your definition. We project our feelings and thoughts onto other people. We assign them to other people to skirt around our own dysfunction or problems. For example, if I'm thinking of being unfaithful in my marriage, I project those thoughts onto my wife, and accuse her of infidelity or flirting with other guys. This allows me to avoid taking responsibility for my own uncomfortable feelings and thoughts. The problem is that I still have issues. While I escaped those uncomfortable feelings and thoughts temporarily, I am still enslaved to them. The better I get at avoiding it, the more challenge I will have to face it.

Rationalization. I was told that rationalization is often called the "sour grapes" defense, from the old Aesop fable about a fox and some grapes. The fox desired the grapes, but they were beyond his reach. Therefore, he told himself that the grapes were probably sour anyway. This rationalization assuaged his pain of not being able to obtain them. He made up a logical reason to escape his failure. We can do the same thing. We attempt to explain away or justify the abusive behavior of the perpetrator. We say, "Dad/mom was abused as a child, too." Or, "She really didn't mean to hurt me. That was the only way she knew to express love." We try to protect ourselves from the heinous truth that the person was bad.

Fantasy. As children, we created an inner world, daydreaming to block out the difficult hurt of the abuse in the real world. We fantasized about having that perfect family, instead of the dysfunctional one we experienced. Daydreaming helped us survive. However, when we rely on the fantasy today to avoid working through the issues, we have problems. We never reach the healing stage, because in our pretend world it already exists.

Intellectualization. Similar to rationalization, we can simply remove or intellectualize the emotion from experiences. We are detached or apathetic when discussing the painful past of abuse. For some of us, it's easier to be distant from these feelings when they are deep and agonizing. We know the words to describe emotions, but we have no comprehension of what we are really feeling.

Denial. We simply deny what has really happened to us.

Repression/Suppression. Out of mind, out of sight! Repression puts painful thoughts and memories out of our minds. We forget them. To some extent, all of the defenses work around this basis. Repression is commonly considered unconsciously forgetting, that is, forgetting and not realizing that you are doing it. You have no conscious memory of the sexual abuse, because you have blocked it off or repressed it.

Suppression is similar. You consciously forget the abuse, or make the choice to avoid thinking about it.

Withdrawal. In withdrawal, we remove ourselves from interactions with the world around, especially from anything that could remind us of painful feelings. At times we may avoid any social interactions, books, television, or the media in general. Withdrawal leads us down a path of loneliness, isolation, and alienation, which actually causes greater pain.

We all have used these types of mechanisms at some time in our lives to protect ourselves when we are troubled. However, we usually come to a point when we face and deal with our problems. When we only rely on these defensive mechanisms, and refuse to address the issues, it becomes unhealthy, damaging and destructive. It becomes impossible to heal and experience our true thoughts and feelings.

Pen Action:

- Which of these defensive mechanisms are you currently using today?

- How damaging are these defensives in your life?

Prayer:

Lord, help me to identify the destructive defensive mechanisms in my life. May I rely on the power of Your promises to provide those things that pertain life and godliness. Your divine power has given me everything I need.

God's Embroidery
Author unknown

When I was a little boy, my mother used to embroidery a great deal. I wold sit at her knee, look up from the floor and ask, what are you doing? She told me that she was embroidering. I told her that it looked like a mess from where I was. As I watched her work from the underside, within the boundaries of the little round hoop that she held in her hand, I complained about it. It sure looked messy from where I sat.

She smiled at me, looked down, and gently said, "My son, you go about your playing for a while, and when I am finished with my embroidery, I will put you on my knee and let you see it from my side."

I wondered why she was using some dark threads along with the bright ones, and why they seemed so jumbled from my view. A few minutes passed, and then I heard Mother's voice say, "Son, come and sit on my knee." I was surprised and thrilled to see a beautiful flower or a sunset. I could not believe it. From underneath it looked so messy.

Then Mother said to me, "My son, from underneath it did look messy and jumbled, but you did not realize that there was a pre-drawn plan on the top. It was a design. I was only following it. Now look at it from my side and you will see what I was doing."

Many times through the years I have looked up to my Heavenly Father and said, "Father, what are You doing?" He has answered, "I am embroidering your life. " I have said, "But it looks like a mess to me. It seems so jumbled. The threads seem so dark. Why can't they all be bright?"

The Father has said, "'My child, you go about your business of doing My business, and one day I will bring you to Heaven and put you on My knee and you will see the plan from My side."

Recover and Reclaim

And looking at them Jesus said to them, "With people this is impossible, but with God all things are possible." Matthew 19:26
As a victim of childhood sexual abuse, you have survived.

As survivors, we have lived life with hurt, pain and confusion. In some cases, we have tried to recover by using fantasy, numbing ourselves and ignoring the abuse ever occurred.. We have adopted compulsive behaviors and addictions like food, drugs, or sex to cope with the aftermath of the abuse. We have become workaholics to cover the pain.

In my personal story I became a martial arts practitioner to foster a sense of safety and peace to both myself and those I taught. Academics, numerous degrees and endless pursuits of studies has been strategies for others. These diversions or distraction as some have labeled them helped us survive to our present stage, therefore I don't think they should be totatlly discredited. In childhood the diversions served as coping skills to deal with the misinformation we learned. However now as adults they often impede recovery. What is recovery? To me recovery is the message of hope.

Many survivors never have heard this message. They believe their life will always be lived through the lens of being damaged goods. This is were the message of Christianity provides hope. You are a child of God, living life, claiming

His promises for yourself, and helping others along the way, with the hope of eternal salvation.

I taught a kids' Bible class. I placed silver dollars in a bucket of ice water. I told the children, "You can keep whatever you pull out of the bucket." By the end of the lesson, their little hands were freezing. I asked them, "Why were you willing to plunge your little hands into the cold, painful, freezing water?" One student said, "Because the money was worth sticking our hands into the cold water." That's what recovery is about! As children of God, we have a great advantage knowing that God is with us.

Recover in the dictionary is often defined as "to get back". Although true, I believe there is a better word we can use: reclaim. Recovery is reclaiming . There is no way we can recover the love we never experienced during our abuse. The time of abuse cannot be physically relived. You cannot transport yourself back in time and say, "Hey! You are supposed to love me and protect me! Stop doing this to me! This is not what love is about! " However, you can reclaim being loved. You can reclaim the ability to love others. You can reclaim boundaries. You can reclaim confidence. You can reclaim God-esteem , self-control, and discipline. Happiness, joy, and peace can be reclaimed through recovery. This recovery doesn't happen overnight. It involves working through the mental, psychological, spiritual issues while rebuilding your character into the image of Christ. Be reasonable and set realistic recovery goals.

Be faithful in small things because it is in them that your faith lies

Mother Teresa of Calcutta

If you have been working through this book, you have already started the reclaiming process. Although this section is called "Recover", you have already begun. The remainder of the text simply provides more opportunities to employ more resources.

Whatever got you to this point to endure and survive deserves respect. Now, as you continue your journey, you must make a conscious decision to work through the issues. You can't work around, over, or under the emotions and feelings of abuse. You have to work through them. The pain generated by the abuse must be confronted. As you continue working through recovery, the pain will not diminish instantaneously. When I went through recovery, I felt worse before getting better. Remember the bucket of freezing cold water? However, it does get better as you move from survivor to living a new life through the power of Jesus Christ.

Moving Forward

For the longest time, I did not understand the idea that before you move forward in recover that you must stand still. Standing still represented being reflective and taking inventory of my current attitudes and assessing how the abuse affected those attitudes toward self and others. Let try a simple exercise. Name the subtle and not so subtle negative messages about your self, body image, worth and value.

1.
2.
3.
4.
5.
6.
7.

Name name the positive messages you hold about yourself, value, image

1.
2.
3.
4.
5.
6.
7.

Was easier and faster to name the negative than the positive? For many surivivors that seems to be the norm. As wounded survivors we often carry around the negative messages and self-abuse. These negative messages are part of our life today. Today, i still am my worst critic. These message are repeated over and over.

- Thomas you can't do anything right.
- You're an idiot. How could you have not seen that.
- You're such a wimp!
- You don't make enough
- What's taking you so long to work through this
- She's never going to like you
- You should have workshops in every state by now.
- You can't trust yourself

Okay please forgive me for being lazy. I wanted to discuss a bit about self-esteem or God esteem might be a better way to described it. However, I just finished writing about it in my other book, "Christians Get Stuck Too!" I'm feeling a bit blocked out. So if you have a chance to pick up that book, please do! I'll say a little. Your self-esteem does not totally come from yourself. It never has and never will. It will be high or low based on the beliefs and messages you internalized from external sources. Esteem is important for survivors because it carries so many possible outcomes: shame, hope, failure, impotence, joy, peace, failure, helplessness, depression, insults, praise and more. Esteem will either continue to perpetuate the negative cycle or accentuate the positive feedback.

Pen Action:

- How do you feel about surrendering control?

- Are you willing to let others help you, others who have experience dealing with this abuse?

- How do you feel about having to experience painful emotions?

- Write down the parts you hope to reclaim. For example, "I would like to reclaim loving relationships with others."

- You cannot change everything at once, but list several aspects you want to start to experience in recovery. Start with small goals. For example, "I want more of a social life. I want to find a trustworthy friend. I want to confront my abuser. I want to be able to tell someone my story. I want to find a workshop or support group."

- Prioritize the level of importance you feel for these goals.

- Which of these goals are realistic and which may be unrealistic? For example, physically confronting a deceased abuser is not realistic.

- I am not to blame for this betrayal again me. It was not my fault! Rewrite the statement here:

-

- God has the power to heal this hurt and betrayal in my life and make me whole! Rewrite the statement here:

Each path to healing takes on a different look, but two requirements common to all are pace and patience. As children, we learned to deny and cover up our emotions, so it will take time to find them once again. This means dusting off some of the cobwebs from the mental bookshelf to reestablish a connection with that part of ourselves that has been dormant. I have noticed that when there is ample safety, trust, and a nonjudgmental environment, the feelings associated with the abuse begin to surface. I can still remember tears at the beginning of my recovery and still today. I felt frightened as thirty years of hurt, and pain bubbled up. I considered this "out of control" for a guy. I thought, "Men don't cry like this. This is totally dangerous. What will people think?" My body shook, I laughed, I cried, I became angry and tired, and I couldn't stop crying for several hours, but man, did it feel great!

When blessed with the proper environment it's easier to express our emotions Being in the right loving environment with a Christian friend, counselor, elder, pastor, or spouse allows the opportunity to use the tears, trembling, and laughing to work through the grief. We often think these outward manifestations are the actual emotion, but serve as the releasing mechanisms of fear, hurt, and grief. Remember the story of Joseph?

Then Joseph could not control himself before all those who stood by him, and he cried, "Have everyone go out from me." So there was no man with him when Joseph made himself known to his brothers. Genesis 45:1

Many of the stories the guys shared in this book started out as simple short statements devoid of much feeling. They were terrified. They didn't know how they would be perceived, believed and accepted by those who listened. One participant mentioned a time when he told his story and it didn't go so well. He believed his fiancé needed to know this part of his history. It was too much for her. The wedding ring never made it on her finger.

Don't Assume

Never make the assumption that everyone can handle your story. If another person is not willing or able to listen, they may have their own issues. You need find someone else. When I needed that ear the most, God provided a wonderful friend who accepted me in a caring, nonjudgmental way. But I had to experience multiple rejections before finding that friend. Too bad Healing Broken Men wasn't around then ☺. Don't give up. Keep trying to develop safe relationships and environments.

As I became more comfortable in a safe environment, my feelings became part of the story. It took years to reach this point and find a friend who was ready to allow me to release. When the appropriate atmosphere was there, the dam broke, and the waters of healing began to flow. I had a time of celebration and rejoicing as barriers and walls of abuse begin to break down. Finally my story was real. I was being validated.

This part of the healing process gives you an opportunity to combat the lie the abuser instilled within you. Let the threats, frights, abandonment begin to evaporate with the sharing of your story. You will need to tell it numerous times. Whenever the safe environment is present, you will probably feel more prompting and ease of release. You will find your voice once again. When you begin to share your story, you might feel a bit ambivalent. Sometimes it feels you as the betrayed have become the betrayer. You might think,

- Who might I hurt in the process in revealing parts of my story?
- Who can I trust?
- Would people still love me if they knew?"
- Am I losing my mind sharing this?

Please understand that you cannot continue to live life like this. God doesn't want you to. He wants you to experience wonderful loving relationships with family and friends. You may feel exhilarated telling your story, then you might feel like an idiot, but don't be afraid. Start to replace the loneliness, isolation, and hurt with healthy God-esteem and interaction with others. Be patient and consistent

Pen Action:

1. List the names of people you feel are part of your safe healing environment. You can use some of the names you have listed in previous exercise.

2. Explain your ideal setting for sharing your story. Is it in a workshop, one-on-one, with a counselor, or with someone else?

If you are going through hell, keep going.
Winston Churchill

3. Write down boundaries of your safe environment. For example, you might say, "Joe, I need a friend who can listen and not be judgmental. Can you do that for me?" Two boundaries are here: listening, and not being judgmental.

4. List things that make you feel uncomfortable or unsafe for sharing your story.

5. Is gender an issue for you? Would you rather share with another guy?

6. Do you have physical boundaries that need respected? For example, are hugs off limits for you?

7. List people you know who would make your healing environment unproductive. They can be critical, can't handle confidential information, etc.

8. If you are married, do you plan to share this with your spouse, if you have not already?

Truths and Promises

Cast your burdens upon the LORD and He will sustain you; He will never allow the righteous to be shaken. Psalm 55:22

But if we hope for what we do not see, with perserverance we wait eagerly for it. But in all these things we overwhelmingly conquer through Him who loved us. For I am convinced that neither death, no life, not angels, nor pirncipalities, nor things present, nor things to come nor powers, nor height, nor depth, nor any other created thing, will be able to separateus form the love of God, which is in Christ Jesus our Lord. *Romans 8:25, 37, 30*

Chapter Seven
Working through Issues

And He has said to me, "My grace is sufficient for you, for power is perfected in weakness." Most gladly, therefore, I will rather boast about my weaknesses, so that the power of Christ may dwell in me. 2 Corinthians 12:9

Does Vulnerability Equal Weakness?

Men have been sold another bill of lies. This one equates vulnerability with weakness. We are socialized and taught that men are knights in shinning armor. If you have ever been on the battlefield, you know that those with shiny armor often represent soldiers who have not been on the field for extended periods. They are rookies. The experienced and seasoned veterans have scars, scuff marks, and dents. These warriors have engaged the enemy. Anytime you expose your self to fight or work through issues it means you are vulnerable. If you believe the macho, self-sufficient role will bring you success, reconsider. The student is not greater than the Teacher.

Is Jesus one of your heroes? Hopefully He is at the top of the list. Think back to the story of the garden of Gethsemane. Gethsemane means "oil press", and Jesus suffered like a ripe olive in the Garden of Gethsemane. We might suppose that

Jesus pouring out his heart only to the Father was sufficient, but that's not the scene. Consider Peter, James and John, They were being asked by their best friend, their Lord, Master, and Teacher, to watch and experience his pain, agony. They are being invited to watch Jesus during his most vulnerable time.

- Was Jesus afraid to be vulnerable?
- Did he equate it with weakness?
- Did he view it as a character flaw?

No. We respect Jesus more when we see him in the Garden. We see the strength of character in risking vulnerability. This is where true strength resides.

Life became bearable for me when I realized that being vulnerable was not the enemy, but a tool for healing. As children we felt helplessly controlled by others through the abuse. In adulthood, we strive with every ounce of our being to control everything, right down to our very emotions. We believe this control means we are in charge of life, and it provides a false comfort and stability that we often equate with safety. It's a lie. How do you learn to set safe boundaries without first taking the risk of being vulnerable? In the big picture the best outlook is the word vulnerable. Once you confront the "**vulner**" then you are "**able**" to start the healing.

Pen Action:

- Write down your greatest fear of being vulnerable.

- Describe what you consider is weak for a man.

- Do you believe that fear is a sign of weakness?

- Watch Mel Gibson's The Passion, the portion with Jesus in the Garden, then write what you think of Jesus being vulnerable and showing His distress, to his close friends

- In your view, what did Jesus lose by showing this emotional side of him?

Have This Attitude

Before going any further, I want to share with you three points of a lesson I preached to at congregations across the country on this subject. The lesson was entitled, "Have this Attitude" from Philippians 2:5. If you remember Jesus during the final hours of His ministry, he washed the disciple's feet, teaching them a valuable lesson that we can learn from.

First, you have nothing to prove, but a destiny to live. We see Jesus, the King of kings, the Lord of lords, in one of the most subservient roles in Jewish culture. Even Jewish slaves did not wash the feet of their friends. The Creator humbled himself before the created. Why? He had nothing to prove. Jesus was very aware and confident in His identity. He was the Son of God How does this apply to you? **You are a child of God**, holy, redeemed, and a new creature. You lay aside the old and put on the new. You do not have anything to prove to the world, but a destiny to live as a child of the King.

Don't let your pride of how others might view you being open and vulnerable hinder your recovery.

Second, you have nothing to lose and everything to gain. Jesus did not have anything to lose because He was given all things by the Father. God has made that promise to us:

Grace and peace be multiplied to you in the knowledge of God and of Jesus our Lord; seeing that His divine power has granted to us everything pertaining to life and godliness, through the true knowledge of Him who called us by His own glory and excellence. *2 Peter 1:2-3*

Unfortunately, we often fail to claim these promises due to fear. We believe handling the issues independently is better or easier than submitting them to God. He has instructed us to lay every care and anxiety on Him. He cares for us.

When I say you have nothing to lose, it does not mean a recovery without effort, pain and disappointments. In my healing, I have experienced rejection, but it turned out to be for the best in the long run. It was difficult to have that perspective in middle of the crisis, but I eventually came around.

Finally, you have nothing to hide, but a love to show. Okay, let's go back to Jesus at the Garden of Gethsemane. Jesus loved the disciples so much that he didn't hide this suffering moments from them. At some point or time during your healing you may experience agonizing hurt, but resist the urge to hide around safe people. Be honest, so you can be lifted up. When I preached this lesson, I shared how grief overwhelmed me, and I had thoughts of suicide. This is not unusual, and I'm not alone. Some of the greatest men in the Bible expressed such thoughts. The congregations were brought to tears as they mourned with me as I shared my story. But through God's power, I conquered. By not hiding my agony, and by being honest with my story, others were lifted up from the edge of suicide., edified and encouraged. I will share this story with you after this section.

Pen Action:

1. List the things in life you feel you need to prove.

2. List the things in life you feel you will lose if you do not confront these issues of abuse.

3. List the things you feel you need to hide in your life. Are these things damaging to you. Are they damaging to others?

Judas Feelings: Suicide

Then the LORD God said, "It is not good for the man to be alone... Genesis 2:18

This is one of those subjects that often is not acknowledged. No one who is a Christian in his right mind would even consider thoughts of suicide...Right?

I used to think that also, until the issues of my abuse surfaced in my life. The emotional pain was so excruciating along with rejection, and feeling unloved, the contemplation of suicide did not phase me. Although a lie, it felt like a solution. If you feel suicidal, call someone now, ask for help now, don't allow yourself to be alone. You just need to make it through today, tomorrow will take care of itself.

Sharing an Experience

Trust is at the root of the intimacy we desire. I can remember balling my eyes out watching those cheesy, Hollywood commercials showing the happy family. I was frustrated that I didn't know how to develop such close relationships with others.

I often misread signals, looking for perfection in my friendships, only to be devastated when they failed. I thought I had failed. As a survivor, you will be elated at your first encounter with affection and trust. It will be memorable. I don't need to tell you that each human connection is valuable and precious. Treasure and nourish each valuable relationship, so each one can flourish. Remember that no one relationship will supply everything you need, so build many relationships with other Christians in the family of God. Reach out and ask others to support you in your endeavor to heal.

Remember, heartaches will likely come. I'll share a personal story with you. I had a friend who had been through the ringer of life. When other abandoned him, guess who was there. When other rejected his taboo issues in faith circles, I continued to standby. Not that he owed me anything, but if I was going through such issues, I know that I would rather have at least one person who I could depend on. I helped him through it. My issues as a survivor were on the table, not all the graphic details, but acknowledged. As he and I talked one evening during dinner, something he said triggered flashbacks of memories I had not recalled before. More faces and abuse me were being revealed. I felt momentarily stunned. It probably showed on my my face.

"Are you okay?" he asked.

"Wow! Can I share this with you?"
He shrugged. "Sure."

"I can't believe it. They passed me from one member to the next like a piece of meat." Tears streamed down my face. It hit me hard.

> Joy and sorrow are inseparable...together they come, and when one sits alone with you...remember that the other is asleep upon your bed.
> Kahlil Gibran

I had previously worked through many other abuse issues, so I accepted this newly revealed fact as yet another part of my story. I moved through the stages of grief in a few minutes.

He scolded me. "That's some serious [crap] you need to deal with. You need help!" There wasn't much conversation after that point. What could I say? I had no idea it was an issue for him. , I related to all the times I had quietly listened to his experiences of hurt and pain. Perhaps he was correct, but when he stopped returning my emails and phone calls, and avoided conversation with me, I felt like I a bug splattered on the grill of a Mack truck driven by my best friend. I later learned that he had always thought of me as a pillar because of his perception of the way I handle issues. However in his eyes, this made me vulnerable. He didn't appreciate that. He had his own issues and equated my openess of emotion and sharing as a sign of weakness. He was always resistant to expressing emotion, afraid he might lose control.

Only later did I realize my friend had similar issues that he could not face, and they triggered a defense mechanism. He was avoiding me personally, because of issues it brought he was afraid to face. Our friendship took several steps backward. Although acquaintances today, the level of friendship, brotherhood and intimacy has never been restored. What does one do when this happens? Respect the boundaries, pray and move on, which is easier said than done after eight years of friendship. The good news is that God opened another door. A few weeks later, another friend, who had been part of my support group, decided he wanted to strengthen our friendship by sharing the difficult along with the easy. Without even knowing what had happened, he asked, "Any more realizations unraveled in your story?" Truly God works in mysterious ways.

Different Reactions

The reason for sharing the story is to share what I learned from this experience. People bring different experiences and perspectives to a relationship. They will react differently to your story. Even close friends may react in hurtful ways, or unintentionally say unproductive things. It's going to happen. I can only express my sadness. Do not let this stop you from working toward healing. Do keep looking for friends who will help you. God will provide them.

Pen Action:
Are you ready to share your story with others?

Prayer:

Lord, please bless my life with friends and loved with whom I can share my experiences and story. Help me to grow for opening heart. When pain is part of the process, stand beside me and strengthen me.

Moving Through Stages

By this point, your emotions are probably like toothpaste; squeezed out and impossible to get back in the tube.. So the process has begun. Dealing with this issue is similar to working through the stages of grief associated with a death and with good reason. Part of you is being put to death, so you can resurrect newness of heart. I recently experienced the death of a parent, and discovered that many of the same stages of grief and acceptance are similar. The Kübler-Ross model describes, in five discrete stages, the process by which people deal with grief and tragedy. It was introduced by Elisabeth Kübler-Ross in her 1969 book "On Death and Dying". I have added a few of my own, based on being a Christian, and using God's word. The stages may not occur in sequential order. For instance, depression for some may precede denial. Each time a new memory or flashback is triggered, I work through these stages. As you become more experienced it will become easier, and the intensity will decrease.

The stages are:
- Denial
- Anger
- Resentment
- Bargaining

- Depression
- Acceptance
- Your Peace
- God's Peace

Denial describes your refusal to believe what happened to you. This denial may be segmented into stages:
- **Fact:** You avoid the facts of the matter. For example, you may have experienced difficulties facing the fact that you were sexually abused by a relative.

- **Responsibility:** You attempt to shift or minimize your responsibility to hold the abusers accountable for their actions. So you make up reasons why they were bad parents, such as, "They were abused as children."

Impact is when you avoid to look at the amount of damage that the abuse has caused in your life. In reality, your view of the world has been distorted. "Well I just got over it and moved on and lived life." In reality, you have simply ignored the impact of the abuse. At some point you need to face the real impact of the damage. People who deny the impact are often harsh, judgmental or angered towards those who acknowledge the impact in their life. For example, a brother might say to another sibling, "What's wrong with you? We were both abused and I'm doing okay. Why bring it up now?"

Anger is not always bad. Even God displays righteous anger. It's defined as a strong feeling of displeasure aroused by a known or perceived wrong or grievance. However, when anger is not addressed, it can develop into bitterness and resentment. Your anger may be directed toward your perpetrator, at others, or the whole world. Like many, you might direct it toward God or even at yourself.

Resentment: I like to define resentment as anger that continues to cycle around in the mind. If not released, resentment grows into bitterness.

Depression often is a cycle of sadness. We lose hope. We become numb to any emotion other than sadness. That is why I believe that Jesus is a crucial key in recovery. He offers hope that is unequal to any other hope. His promises are sure if we are willing to follow.

Bargaining is a similar type of denial. We want to believe that our problem of abuse is not really that horrible. We attempt to minimize it by saying, "Tom's abuse was worst than mine! What I went through was nothing compared to him..." Unfortunately, I find some counselors, preachers, and pastors believe this philosophy. If it's bothering you, it's an issue. The same boulder hurts one man and crushes the other. Even God understands that if it's bothering you, it has power in your life, and is no small issue. God tells us to cast it upon Him, because He cares for us, and can handle it.

Acceptance is the stage in which you acknowledge the abuse that happened to you is real. It cannot be changed. It is fact.

Your Peace is the stage of acceptance in which you work through the issues of abuse, and experience healing and recovery.

God's Peace transcends anything you could ever experience or explain. It is the peace that He promised to leave with His children. It is a spiritual peace. It is the knowledge that, no matter how many times you have to work through these stages, He will never leave you nor forsake you. He will heal the years of hurt that the abuse has produced and bless you with the abundant life here, and in the world to come.

Moving On

Not that I have already obtained it or have already become perfect, but I press on so that I may lay hold of that for which also I was laid hold of by Christ Jesus. Brethren, I do not regard myself as having laid hold of it yet; but one thing I do: forgetting what lies behind and reaching forward to what lies ahead, I press on toward the goal for the prize of the upward call of God in Christ Jesus. *Philippians 3:12-14*

The Dark Candle by Strickland Gillilan, Aspiring to Greatness

"A man had a little daughter--an only and much-beloved child. He lived for her ~ she was his life. So when she became ill and her illness resisted the efforts of the best obtainable physicians, he became like a man possessed, moving heaven and earth to bring about her restoration to health.

His best efforts proved unavailing and the child died. The father was totally irreconcilable. He became a bitter recluse, shutting himself away from his many friends and refusing every activity that might restore his poise and bring him back to his normal self. But one night he had a dream. He was in Heaven, and was witnessing a grand pageant of all the little child angels. They were marching in an apparently endless line past the Great White Throne. Every white-robed angelic tot carried a candle. He noticed that one child's candle was not lighted. Then he saw that the child with the dark candle was his own little girl. Rushing to her, while the pageant faltered, he seized her in his arms, caressed her tenderly, and then asked: "How is it, darling that your candle alone is unlighted?"Father, they often relight it, but your tears always put it out." Just then he awoke from his dream. The lesson was crystal clear, and its effects were immediate. From that hour on he was not a recluse, but mingled freely and cheerfully with his former friends and associates.

It's time to crucify the old, beat up, scarred, fearful, anxious self, and work to attain the happy, confident, joyful person that Jesus offers you. Press on!

Therapy Isn't a Bad Word

In the Christian community, the words "therapy" or "counseling" can be very intimidating, perhaps because we associate doctors, psychiatrists, and clinics with these words. We have been sold the lie that we are self-sufficient and can solve our own problems. God has created dependency upon each other. We need each other. We need interdependence. Do you picture of therapy as lying on a leather couch, while a psychiatrist asks you cold, personal questions? Please erase this scenario from your mind. Within the church community, recovery can be experienced with loving, caring Christian counselors and therapists, as well as friends and family, who know biblical principles and methods for helping you to be victorious. First you must relinquish some factors of pride and myth:

You are your own man. You don't need help. If that's true, you should be able to do anything on your own. You can fix your microwave, fill your own cavities, service your own car, and invest in the stock market. The fact is you cannot solve every problem by yourself. You need to seek out people who have experience, expertise, or education in a certain field.

People will think I'm wacko. The problem with this view is that, once again, pride enters into the picture. "Pride comes before the fall". You are equating working through issues, and rebuilding your life, as shameful and negative. Working to better and improve your situation is not wrong, but wise.

Someone is directing my life. Really!, you have a fear of control—or not being in control. . It's the old power struggle. You are being expected to share thoughts and experiences which make you feel vulnerable. So this gives you a sense of someone having authority over you. Think of it from this perspective instead. You are working with a counselor or friend at your own pace. Life was so bad for me when I was in this spot, that whatever was shared with me, I gobbled it up and used it. You are willingly submitting parts of your life to God and others who can help you heal. This is difficult, and it's one reason that during the small group breakouts we share our experiences.

Therapy is expensive. When conducting the three day workshops, I often hear this. My only reply is, "Freedom and transformation comes with a price! You must decide how important this is to you. Some give all they have to be free. What you are willing to sacrifice" If you feel your therapist, counselor is in it only for the money, find someone you believe is genuine.

Submitting to therapy means I'm a failure. If you have the opportunity to get well, but do not try, then you have failed. Failure is not written in ink, but pencil.

Confronting the Abuser

Should you confront your abuser? This is a difficult question to address. Each person must determine for himself the answer to it. Usually it's not a good idea. However, if you decide it is necessary, you must consider your motive and purpose for initiating a confrontation. Is it in your best interest? Is the person still abusing others?

In my own experience with one of my abusers, I initiated a confrontation, first through letter, and then with a follow-up phone call. What did I want from him? I wanted a simple acknowledgement of his betrayal, and to show some type of remorse for putting me through a living hell. What did I receive? Denial!

He denied that it had ever happened. I didn't receive the answer I desired. However, I still felt empowered acknowledging it to him. Now it's on his plate.

Confrontation might be difficult if the abuser has moved away or died, but it's not necessary to meet face to face to receive the benefits of confrontation. In most cases, the abuser will not have the ability to answer your question of "Why me?" Secondly, he will have no understanding of what you have experienced and struggled with all these years. The point is, don't get your hopes up that physcial confrontation will help matters!

Seek other methods to work with the issue especially if you face the possibility of destruction to your recovery progress, physical harm, or emotional harm. After all, confrontation is simply a method of standing up for yourself, and to the abuse that you suffered. Confrontation can bring up scores of other issues to be dealt with, so prepare beforehand. Make sure you have shared your story with others and have figured out some of the details and the feelings attached to the betrayal. Make sure you have had an opportunity to share with other survivors and build a supportive network.

Confrontation may reaffirm several facts for you:

- A wrongful abusive act was committed.
- This person is held accountable to God.
- You are not responsible for this person's betrayal.
- No one, especially you, deserves this type of treatment.

Methods to enact confrontation

Role playing is one of the most powerful tools you can use. It allows you the opportunity to rehearse scenarios in which you actually confront your perpetrator without fear of harm or danger. Use friends or members of your support group. This will enable you to experience various reactions and responses. If you are not ready to use real people, start with a life size poster, the ones you can get from movie theaters. (They are available after the movie promotion is over.) When role playing with others, be sure to have them act out scenarios you don't want, but may experience anyway. Scenarios like: the abuser denies anything, he shifts the blame elsewhere, he accuses you of just causing trouble, so he simply shows no remorse. Other scenarios can include the abuser wanting reconciliation and begging forgiveness.

Guided hypnotherapy is another way of confronting the abuser. If your therapist is skilled in this art, it may serve as another tool to heal. I was a bit skeptical when I was first introduced to this technique, until I understood it was a form of meditation combined with some positive symbols. It isn't witchcraft, black magic, or mind tampering. It is similar to the martial arts practice of breathing and focusing, working with the subconscious mind.

Writing a letter is another means of confronting. Write down your thoughts and feelings toward the abuser. You may not actually mail it. Write this letter numerous times, until you are able to articulate what you want to say. After you finish your final version, copy it to your journal. This exercise will help you to find that voice within you. If you ever do decide to conduct an actual face-to-face or phone confrontation, the letter will provide you with the exact words you desire to express. Read the letter to a friend, counselor, or pastor. If the perpetrator is dead, you may want to visit the grave and read the letter at the gravesite. You could also speak to an old picture of the person. This may all feel stupid at first, but each time you tell your story, and release those feelings, you are closer to your goal of closure.

Forgiveness or Vengeance

> 'The LORD is slow to anger and abundant in lovingkindness, forgiving iniquity and transgression; but He will by no means clear the guilty, visiting the iniquity of the fathers on the children to the third and the fourth generations.' *Numbers 14:18*

Let's be real, now! You have probably thought about revenge at some point in your life. Feelings of revenge can be scary. It's difficult because the world tells us that revenge is okay--as long as we don't act on it. I totally disagree. I find revenge destructive. It leads to regression, not recovery. I believe only

God can provide peace, because He says, "Vengeance is mine and I will repay!"

If you understand that God is just, fair and righteous, you know that He is a God who accomplishes what He promises. You may actually feel a bit sad for your abuser, because it is a dreadful thing to fall into the hands of the living God in a sinful unrepentant state. Sometimes in the church community, we gloss over the concept of hell fire, but hell has its place. It is the only way a just God can repay the rebellious, stubborn, unrepentant abuser who committed such an atrocity to an innocent pure child.

Since God takes care of vengeance, let's talk about forgiveness. We often use the old adage, "Forgive and forget". The concept of forgiveness has taken on a different concept for me. I had been taught that forgiving meant never remembering what had been done to me. This was an impossible task because something would trigger a flashback of the sexual abuse. Unless I had a lobotomy or amnesia, forgetting was not an option. It tortured me. How could I be a Christian if I couldn't really "forgive and forget" this abuse?

God truly provides an answer when we are seeking with our whole heart.
.
Truly, forgiveness is a divine attribute.

Studying this topic helped me realize that forgiveness is a choice that one has to make. When I forget something, it has slipped my mind, perhaps by accident, or due to distraction. In contrast, forgiveness means I have rightful claim to retribution and punishment against my abuser, but I choose to relinquish it and give it up to God.

This didn't erase the fact that the abuse occurred, nor that the abuse was wrong. It meant that God had granted me the power to be like Him, to pardon sin, and to stop feeling the resentment for a wrong perpetrated against me. In other words, the forgiveness was for me, not my abuser. God knows the heart of my abuser and will meter out any justice in His time

Forgiving meant I had to release the pent up anger and revenge in my heart, allowing God to release the pressure.

- Did it mean I needed to drop my boundaries and have dinner with my abuser?
- Did it mean I needed to send him a card on his birthday? No.
- Did it mean I had to build a close friendly relationship with him? No!

Sin carries a penalty according to Scripture . The penalty is death. When God wipes out the sinful acts I have committed against Him, He chooses to relinquish the just penalty and retribution that my actions deserve. I also need to relinquish the just penalty done against me and leave it for God. Forgivenss is a process. It's something you'll continually be exposed to.

In Relationship with a God I Don't Know Yet

A relationship with God is the key to thriving. It offers you an everlasting relationship that literally transcends time. You are created in His image. He ascribes to you a value that can never be diminished or taken by others, it is one reason the sanctity of life is so important, because His gives each life value.

If the God factor is new to you, and you have no exposure of knowledge of this subject, then let me take a few moments and share with you my understanding of beginning a relationship with God and my personal conversion. It's a bit simplified yet awesome and exilirating. Feel free to send me email if you have questions.

In the beginning, God created the universe and everything that exists: angels, man, animals, bugs, fish, birds, stars, moons, planets, light, energy, water, dirt, air, trees, and food . Do you get the picture? In the beginning, God created the heavens and the earth (Genesis 1:1). God created everything in six days, pronounced it good, and rested on the seventh day.

The crowning glory of his earthly creation was man and woman. They were different from all other earthly creatures. They were different from the whales, sheep, and monkeys. They were created in God's image. Adam and Eve had free will and a moral responsibility. They could love, think, and understand. They could express joy, kindness, and peace. They could freely communicate with God. (Genesis 1:26-31). There were no barriers between them and God; they were in perfect relationship with Him.

God gave all the other earthly creatures instincts. He gave people the ability to love.

Love is defined as doing what is in the best interest of the person or object loved. God's rule to mankind, Adam and Eve, was to not eat from the tree of the knowledge of good and evil in the middle of the garden. They could eat from any other tree in the garden, but not this one (Genesis 2:16-17). Obedience meant they loved God by doing what He requested (John 14:15). How else would you show your love to someone who created you, gave you everything you needed, and gave you charge over the entire planet?

We have no idea how long these two people lived in the garden before Satan showed up. Satan, a spiritual being, is known as the great deceiver of mankind. Somewhere along the way, he decided to rebel and go against God's will. He convinced other spiritual beings to follow his lead. The name Satan means, "Adversary". His disobedience to God's rule meant that he did not love God. For some reason, Satan and his followers decided to be bad, to be evil. As such, they are adversaries of God.

One day, while in the garden, Satan deceived Eve and told her a bold-faced lie. God told Adam and Eve they would die on the day they disobey and ate the fruit from the forbidden tree. Satan twisted this command and appealed to mankind's vanity to be like God (Genesis 3:4-6). Eve ate the fruit and shared it with her husband Adam. Sin--which is disobedience to God's rule--became part of this earthly world.

Two types of death entered into the life of mankind: physical death and spiritual death. Death simply means separation. Adam and Eve began to die physically. They got old and wrinkly. Even worse, their spirits no longer had direct communication or relationship with God because of their sin.

God is holy. This righteous attribute keeps Him from tolerating the continual practice of sin, evil, and disobedience. He has no experience with sin, because He always does what is right and good. He is the standard. With sin comes the price of death (Romans 6:23). Once we sin, we become sinners and are separated from God (Ezekiel 18:20-28, Isaiah 59:1-2). Each person is held responsible for his own sin. Sin itself is not passed on to others, but its consequences are. We did not inherit Adam's actual sin that he personally committed against God, but we did reap the consequences of his sin, physical death. We all physically die as a consequence of Adam's sin. However, our separation from God is due to our own individual sin (Romans 5:12, 3:23). We all understand this principle. For example, your father may have been an alcoholic. You are not labeled as an alcoholic because of his weakness, but you suffered the consequences of his alcoholism, such as seeing your family broken apart.

A time comes when innocence is lost and we sin against God. It is at that point we are sinners and we are separated from God in the spiritual sense, spiritual death. We are lost. Because God loves us so much, and desires a relationship with us, He developed a plan that would restore our relationship with Him. The history of the world revolves around this plan. Jesus the Messiah, God in a human body, came to pay the price of death for sin (Ephesians 1:3-4). He went about doing good. He healed the sick, raised the dead and taught the truth. Yet His greatest work meant taking on our sin suffering a brutal death that you and I deserved. He was buried. Then Jesus conquered death with His resurrection.

Jesus payment of death is only for those who will receive it, and choose to obey Him (John 1:12-13). This is a decision each person must make. Jesus is the head of the church , also called the kingdom (Matthew 16:18). This kingdom will one day be delivered to the Father in heaven (1 Corinthians 15:20-26). So how do we become part of the kingdom? Let's take a look at some examples of people who became part of the spiritual kingdom that Jesus built. Please read Acts chapter two. Here are Jewish people represented from various nations in the world. Peter preaches the good news concerning Jesus Christ. He explains that Jesus lived for us, died for us, was buried, and God raised Him again. When the people believed this, they were convicted, and they asked Peter, "What shall we do?" Peter told them, "Repent and each one of you be baptized for the forgiveness of sins (Acts 2:37-41)." (Baptism is the Greek word meaning to dip, plunge beneath, or immerse. It is a part of the new beginning. Like Jesus we are buried and arise to a new life. (Romans 6:1-10, 1 Peter 3:21-22). This is a brief summary. Please search and read the Scriptures and let your salvation be based upon God's word and not just what I say. Let me share with you my conversion.

In my teen years there came a point where I had to relinquish my own will and submit to God's will. I had heard the word of God, knew all the Bible stories about Jesus and how he had died for me. I believed it in my heart, but wasn't ready to give Him control. I was in control. I resisted any idea of repentance, turning from my idea of truth to God's truth.

Compared to the teens in my neighborhood, I was already a saint. One day, I allowed the bad influences to pressure me into committing a mischievous crime. Most people would consider it nothing. We were simply being teenagers, but something inside me said, "You are being evil, You are just like the rest of them. Hurting others and doing bad things." Being trained to discern right and wrong behavior was the pits. It brought guilt and remorse that weighed me down. No matter what my friends thought, I knew I had violated a law above and beyond my little self righteous rules and grieved the heart of the God who loved me so much. Life changed.

I decided to stop living life by my flawed rules and urges and follow what God had laid out for living the best life. I knew it was going to be difficult. Now my so called posse would reject me. They would ridicule and harass me for choosing to walk a different path. They would no longer watch my back, the black sheep. In spite of them, I walked down the aisle that cold wintery night and confessed my allegiance to Jesus

Christ. There was no heat in that little church that evening. The waters were freezing cold. I knew what needed to be done. I had to follow the example and pattern to submit to God and allow Him to wash sin from my soul so I could arise from that cold freezing water to walk a new life.

Scared Boys Terrified Men

A Final Word

I want to encourage you, support you, and express my admiration. You have embarked on launching your healing journey. You are doing something!

I celebrate the day when you look behind you, and realize that, with the help of God, friends, family and perseverance your vast ocean of pain has been reduced to a mere puddle, which evaporates in the sunlight of the Son.

That's a bit of cheesy. Let me say simply, "I send my brotherly Christian love to all those who are working through the issues of sexual abuse."

Feel free to drop me an email or letter. I would love to hear from you www.healingbrokenmen.com

Healing Broken Men
PO Box 123
Bothell, WA 98041

Thomas Edward serves as a Christian life coach and facilitates faith based male survivor workshops based in Seattle, Washington. As a survivor of childhood sexual abuse himself, he's tenacious in educating faith communities and developing resources for male survivors. Thomas started Healing Broken Men ministry around 2001. He believes that providing a safe environment to help male survivors begin to shatter the silence and work towards reclaiming their life in Christ. This is crucial. Thomas is currently working on another master's degree in Psychology and Counseling at Antioch University. His other books include "Christians Get Stuck Too, and Healing a Man's Heart"

References

Feinauer, L. L., Mitchell, J., Harper, J.M., & Dane, S. (1996). The impact of hardiness and severity of childhood sexual abuse on adult adjustment. The American Journal of Family Therapy, 24(3), 206–214.

Filipas, H. H., & Ullman, S. E. (2006). Child sexual abuse, coping responses, self-blame, posttraumatic stress disorder, and adult sexual revictimization. Journal of Interpersonal Violence, 21(5), 652–672.

Finkelhor, D. (1990). Early and long-term effects of child sexual abuse: An update. Professional Psychology: Research and Practice, 21, 325–330.

Fondacaro, K. M., Holt, J. C., & Powell, T. A. (1999). Psychological impact of childhood sexual abuse on male inmates: The importance of perception child abuse & neglect. Child Abuse & Neglect, 23(4), 361–369.

Gartner, R. B. (1999). Betrayed as boys: The psychodynamic treatment of sexually abused men. New York: Guilford Press.

Gartner, R. B. (1999). Relational aftereffects in manhood of boyhood sexual abuse. Journal of Contemporary Psychotherapy, 29(4), 319-353.

Gilgun, J. F., & Reiser, E. (1990). The development of sexual identity among
men sexually abused as children. Families in Society, 71, 515–523.

Goldberg, D. P., & Hillier, V. F. (1979). A scaled version of the General Health Questionnaire. Psychological Medicine, 9, 139–145.

Goldney, R. D., Wilson, D., Dal Grande, E., Fisher, L. J., & McFarlane, A. C. (2000). Suicidal ideation in a random community sample: Attributable risk due to
depression and psychosocial and traumatic events. Australian and New Zealand Journal of Psychiatry, 34, 98–106.

Grossman, F. K., Sorsoli, L., & Kia-Keating, M. (2006). A gale force wind: Meaning making by male survivors of childhood sexual abuse. American Journal of Orthopsychiatry, 76(4), 434-444.

Holmes, G. R., Offen, L., & Waller, G. (1997). See no evil, hear no evil, speak no evil: Why do relatively few male victims of childhood sexual abuse receive help for abuse-related issues in adulthood? Clinical Psychology Review, 17(1), 69-88.

.Kendall-Tackett, K.A.; Williams, L.M.; Finkelhor, D. "Impact of sexual abuse on children : A review and synthesis of recent empirical studies." Psychological Bulletin. v. 113 p. 164–180. 1993

Kia-Keating, M., Grossman, F. K., Sorsoli, L., & Epstein, M. (2005). Containing and resisting masculinity: Narratives of renegotiation among

resilient male survivors of childhood sexual abuse. Psychology of Men &
Masculinity, 6, 169–185.

Hunter, M. (1990c). Abused boys: The neglected victims of sexual abuse.
Lexington, MA: Lexington Books.

Relational Challenges and Recovery Processes in Male Survivors of Childhood Sexual Abuse. Kia-Keating, Maryam; Sorsoli, Lynn; Grossman, Frances K. Journal of Interpersonal Violence vol. 25 issue 4 April 2010. p. 666-683

Lew, M. (2004). Victims no longer: The classic guide for men recovering from sexual child abuse (2nd ed.). New York: Quill

Lisak, D. (1994). The psychological impact of sexual abuse: Content analysis of interviews with male survivors. Journal of Traumatic Stress, 7(4), 525–548.

Luterek, J. A., Harb, G. C., Heimberg, R. G., & Marx, B. P. (2004). Interpersonal rejection
sensitivity in childhood sexual abuse survivors. Journal of Interpersonal Violence, 19(1),
90-107.

Nasjleti, M. "Suffering in silence : The male incest victim." Child Welfare. v. 59 p. 269–275. 1980

Mendel, M. P. (1995). The male survivor: The impact of sexual abuse. Thousand Oaks, California: Sage.

Sorsoli, L., Kia-Keating, M., & Grossman, F. K. (2008). "I keep that hush hush": An in-depth analysis of male survivors' non-disclosure of childhood sexual abuse. Journal of Counseling Psychology, 55(3), 333-345.

Terr, L. (1990). Too scared to cry: Psychic trauma in childhood. New York: Basic Books.

85.Vander Mey, B.J. "The sexual victimization of male children : A review of previous research." Child Abuse & Neglect. v. 12 p. 61–72. 1988

CPSIA information can be obtained at www.ICGtesting.com
Printed in the USA
BVOW022159090912

299889BV00007B/33/P